SHALOM:

The Bible's Word for Salvation, Justice, and Peace

by Perry B. Yoder

Evangel Publishing House
Nappanee, Indiana 46550

Originally published by Faith and Life Press, Newton, Kansas, ISBN: 0-87303-120-2 as Institute of Mennonite Studies Series Number 7. The Institute of Mennonite Studies is the research agency of Associated Mennonite Biblical Seminaries, Elkhart, Indiana 46517-1999.

Design by John Hiebert

ISBN: 0-916035-91-3
Library of Congress Catalog Card Number: 98-72657

Printed in the United States of America
EP 4 3 2

To Myrna Arceo, Arche Ligo, and Carlos Abesamis, S. J.,

who helped me see another world.

Contents

Prologue 1

1. Shalom: Center of Our Faith 3

2. Shalom: The Bible's Peace 10

3. Justice Is Basic 24

4. Salvation: Shalom Justice in Action 39

5. The Atonement: An Act of God's Justice 53

6. Law: Instrument for Shalom Justice 71

7. The State, Shalom, and Justice 85

8. The Prophets, the State, and Shalom 102

9. Jesus: the Messiah of God 120

10. Shalom Making Today 136

Indexes 147

The Writer 154

Prologue

This book grew, initially, from material presented in a biblical theology class at Bethel College in the spring of 1984. Our goal was to discover how shalom might be connected to other biblical themes like creation, salvation, and eschatology.

After I had written the first draft, our family spent four months in the Philippines. I wanted to dialogue about *peace* in a third-world context of poverty, oppression, and struggle for change. (This was during the Marcos regime.) But more importantly, I wanted to experience and promote personal solidarity with poor and oppressed people in such a situation.

My experiences were shattering and shaping. It was not so much a matter of new thoughts, but seeing the world through different eyes with my new friends. As a result, the original draft was greatly revised. In the following pages, you will discover the interplay between my experiences in the Philippines and the development and thrust of the manuscript.

In this book, I am not primarily interested in the topic of violence versus nonviolence. (That ground has been covered many times; I shall, however, return to it briefly in the last chapter.) Instead, my primary concern is with how the Bible talks about and describes peace and how this notion of peace is connected with other core beliefs which we find in the Bible.

Since peace and avoidance of violence are sometimes equated in English, it might be helpful to show how I intend to use the word *peace*. As we develop our inquiry into the Bible, we will discover that peace has a much wider meaning than lack of overt violence. I will therefore use peace in this much broader sense as a goal for which we should strive. However, in my introductory first chapter, in order to lay out more clearly the context and purpose of my work, I will simply echo what I see to be a common concept of peace.

The relation of peace and nonviolence has been a troubling one for me. On the one hand, it seems clear that peace does mean solidarity, good relationships, and absence of violence. On the other hand, I have been convinced for some years that an equation of peace with the avoidance, personally or corporately, of doing physical violence should make sense in terms of our international context. But often it does not, since those who teach nonparticipation in violence often come from affluent nations and from the middle class. Their affluence is in part the result of the violence of exploitation elsewhere. Further, in my experience, those who want to avoid violence often do not actively address or help end the violence of exploitation which would make counterviolence by the oppressed unnecessary. As a result, even peace activism can focus on certain types of violence done by certain groups, for example, the use of nuclear weapons by the military, while ignoring other kinds of violence.

For example, as an American whose country's policies have supported in the Philippines an unjust and exploitive situation for our benefit and to the detriment of the Filipino people, it was hard, if not impossible, for me to talk about peace, let alone speak against violence, with most Filipinos.

In reflecting on this experience, it seemed to me that we who advocate pacifism and nonviolence have perhaps focused too often on means and not enough on the end, on what peace is to be, on our goal. We have become too involved with criticizing violence and not enough involved with peacemaking—working to transform the present structures of injustice and violence into structures of peace and equity. As a result, a central concern of this book is to awaken people to a vision—what it means to be working for peace—and to urge people (myself included) to get on with it.

Thus, this book is devoted more to what ought to be than to how we get there. I hope to evoke a common vision toward which all Christians can and should work. I also hope that those who say they are for peace will become active, sincerely transforming violent and oppressive structures. I recognize that many people are already active, often putting themselves on the line for peace. I hope that in some small way what follows may bolster their efforts and encourage many more to join them.

PERRY B. YODER

1. *Shalom: center of our faith*

P *eace is a middle-class luxury*, perhaps even a Western middle-class luxury. This I experienced during the time I spent in the Philippines, trying to see how peace looked through the eyes of others, especially the eyes of the oppressed. I quickly discovered that they saw advocacy for peace as support for their oppression or, at best, only a cosmetic modification of it. They saw it as opposing those struggling to transform their lives. Because the present system worked, on the one hand, mainly for the benefit of the West and the middle and upper classes and, on the other hand, for the continued poverty of the rest, it seemed clear to them that peace was a luxury they could not afford. Their concern was whether or not they could afford the essentials: rice for today! Talking of peace in this context sounded like the language of oppression used by oppressors to keep the oppressed in their place!

Why was advocating peace in the Philippines so easily seen as support for an unjust cause? Such an understanding of peace grows from two considerations. First, it shows that peace is taken to mean avoiding physical violence, refraining personally from lethal force, and standing against those who use such overt violence.

In the midst of third-world oppression, this type of peacemaking is understood to be against the use of violence to change the existing social and economic order. It seems impossible to the oppressed, who bear the weight of the present order, that these present economic and political structures will be lifted from their shoulders without struggle and violence. From their point of view, they see peace advocates as useless idealists, and, in fact, as standing tacitly against change and for the present order which makes the getting of rice a daily concern. Peace, it seems to them, is the rhetoric of those who have.

Second, and more importantly, this equation of peace as the opposite of the use of lethal violence and which condemns attempts to change the status quo by this force seems perverse to oppressed peoples. They, after all, feel daily the violence of the status quo and see the benefits of this violence accruing to the very people who preach nonviolence to them: westerners and their own middle class and elite. They experience the present social-economic order as oppressive and murderous—leaving many landless, homeless, hungry, and, above all, in deadly fear and voiceless about their destiny. Attempts by them to change this situation are met with harsh repression leading in many cases to torture and summary execution. In such a context, to tell the victims of violence that they should respond peacefully is, to put the best face on it, seen as talking to the wrong people. Their reaction, if it is violent, is only a reaction to the violence which is being done to them. And they ask: is it not those people who, while advocating nonviolence for us, benefit, at least indirectly, from the violence which victimizes us daily?

A common illustration is of a big bully coming up and grabbing someone by the arm and beginning to drag him off. If the victim at this point starts to hit the bully, is he the one who ought to be told about peace? Is it not the bully who first ought to be admonished to let his victim go? Is this not doubly the case for those who are profiting from the bully's actions?

While I was in the Philippines, a palm oil processing plant owned by Guthrie, a British company, was raided. The New People's Army, a revolutionary military force, entered the plant one night, tied up the security guards, took them away, and then destroyed the plant. Violent, to be sure. However, the background to the story is that Guthrie is said to have hired a notorious group of mercenary soldiers to help the company persuade peasant farmers to sell their land to Guthrie so that they could convert a sizable area into a palm plantation. This was done, and the plant was built to process the palm oil. As a result of Guthrie's expansion, many poor farmers lost their land and thus their means of livelihood. The farmers tried various forms of organization and sabotage, but the military used harsh measures to keep order.

From this story, it is easy to understand why the New People's Army is looked upon as the friend of the people, while the government and military, armed, trained, and supported by the United States, are seen as their enemy. After all, the military supports, directly aids, and profits from a system which causes small farmers to lose land, livelihood for support of family, and even life itself. Who in this situation is responsible for violence? To whom should the message of peace and the avoidance of violence be addressed—to those working for justice or those working against it? In this situation, why is it that the advocates of peace, like the church, seem more ready to address their message to the victims of violence and their allies like the New People's Army than to perpetrators of violence like Guthrie?

Now for many who equate peace with doing no violence, this story becomes an occasion for a moral argument. They point out that two wrongs don't make a right, one act of violence does not justify another.

Such arguments make sense to people who own property, whose stomachs are full, who control, to some extent, their own destiny, and who profit from the policies of companies like Guthrie. These arguments are not understood by people who have been deprived of their land and livelihood by violence and are kept in line by violence. Another case of blaming the victim?

All of these factors speak eloquently to the poor and oppressed in the Philippines, and I presume elsewhere, for seeing peace as a middle class, Western luxury, because after all it is they who benefit from the peace of the status quo. It is they who apply their notion of peace to the victims of violence. Yet for the poor and powerless, the experience of violence goes on day after day. At bottom, then, for all of these reasons, peace is easily equated with inaction and no change because in their experience peace seems to live comfortably with the violence of injustice.

Shalom making rather than selective violence

In contrast to this understanding of peace, the major thesis of this book is that shalom, biblical peace, is squarely against injustice and oppression. Indeed, we shall argue that shalom demands a transforming of unjust social and economic orders. Rather than being a message addressed to victims, shalom acts against oppressors for the sake of victims. In the Bible, shalom is a vision of what ought to be and a call to transform society. This clearly implies, as we shall see, that the first contrast is not between shalom and violence, but between shalom and injustice since it is the violence of injustice which is a major block to the coming of shalom. Thus, the equation of peace with nonviolence is, from a biblical standpoint, only partly true; indeed, insofar as peace is understood only as avoiding violence this misrepresents the biblical message of peace.

This understanding is a far cry from seeing peace as the passive avoidance of deadly violence. To me, that is the challenge for peacemaking today: to define peacemaking positively as being for something, rather than negatively as being against something! Otherwise, might it not continue to seem to the third-world poor that *the position of doing no overt violence is really not a peace position at all but support for selective violence? It is against violence by the oppressed but apparently comfortable with violence and injustice by the oppressors.*

Now, in fairness, it is true that for many people committed to biblical peacemaking and nonviolence this is not new. They recognize that peacemaking involves active opposition to and transformation of the structures of oppression and exploitation. In this regard, the portrayal above is a caricature. But it is one which exists in the minds and hearts of many who are oppressed and struggling to end that oppression. Thus, it seems to me that credible peacemaking needs substantial displays of action which directly address the problems just mentioned. Through direct, visible action, witness can be given that peace and nonviolence are not a cop-out. It is this dimension of sustained and serious effort for change which I find an essential part of the biblical notion and message of peace.

Militarism that supports an unjust status quo

The present state of affairs also shows how deadly a second major understanding of peace can be: the peace-through-strength position. In this view, it is thought that military strength will establish and preserve peace. Peace is again equated with lack of conflict. However, in this view, violence is avoided not by practicing some form of violence avoidance but by being strong enough to prevent violence. If we have enough military might, no battles need be fought. As a result, the way to peace is to preserve the no-war status quo by overwhelming military might. Arming for massive destruction is peacekeeping.

In reality, however, as we observe the use of military force around the world, such strength is being used actively to maintain an unjust and oppressive status quo and to stifle those who would change the situation. Peace through strength, as it is experienced by its victims, is oppression through violence, as the corpses, tortured bodies, and hopeless eyes attest in El Salvador, Guatemala, Chile, and the Philippines. In no way is this shalom. It is rather violence for the benefit of oppressors and those who live from the gains of oppression.

As we shall note in the next chapter, our world sees peace as the avoidance of violence which is maintained by force. This view is in tension with the biblical view of peace—shalom as the abolishment of the structures of oppression and violence.

We began by saying that peace is a middle-class luxury. I hope it is now clear why this is so for so many people in the world. I also hope it will become clear that shalom, however, is much needed by the poor, the oppressed, and the dispossessed. This book is in part an argument and an appeal to give up a luxury for a necessity, to give up peace for shalom! It is offered with the hope that the biblical message can revitalize and move Christians to *authentic shalom action—when viewed by those who are not now experiencing shalom.*

I also hope that this book will be useful for those who have given up on peace because they see it as the language of the status quo which plays into the hands of oppressors. The vision of shalom is a vision for the poor and oppressed. It is good news around which all Christians who are committed to the struggle for justice can unite in a witness to their faith. In this sense, the present essay is intended to serve as a bridge between those who are committed to biblical faith and shalom in the first world and in the third world.

Since this book is intended to move to action, at the end we shall consider the question of violence and whether the transformation called for by shalom can or should take place by violent means. This discussion belongs at the end, because violence or nonviolence, if it is to be compatible with shalom, must be shalom producing, and make sense in the context of a struggle for shalom.

This is a very important point. The usual procedure for basing a peace position or teaching on Scripture is to use the Scriptures to provide a positive argument for avoiding violence and to condemn lethal, physical violence. Such a process has a basic flaw—it begins with a definition of what peace in the Bible is, namely nonparticipation in active violence. This equation short-circuits the enterprise since we are then trying to use the Bible to support our own understanding and definition of peace. As we shall see, this can leave other aspects of peace underemphasized or neglected altogether. Consequently, our first task is first to find the biblical understanding of peace, shalom. Then, at the end, we can decide whether shalom and violence are compatible.

A new look at the core of biblical faith

A basic assumption of this book in discovering the meaning of shalom is that at the core of biblical faith lies a cluster of key convictions—beliefs about God, the world, and humankind. These convictions are connected to each other and, in fact, flow into one another. This means that to understand any one of them properly, it is necessary to see how it is linked to other core beliefs and how it is to be understood in light of these connections.

So, we must ask about shalom: how is it connected with other core aspects of biblical faith: justice and salvation, for example; and how does it relate to what we see of God in Jesus? This wider understanding is necessary for a rich and authentic grasp of the biblical notion of shalom. Within the scope of this book, we will not have space to grapple with all of these core convictions, nor to show at every turn how shalom is linked to them. Rather, we are providing only an outline map: how shalom relates to some of the central biblical themes.

The counterpart of this process for understanding shalom is that other aspects of biblical faith also receive part of their meaning from how they are connected with shalom. As we will see, they take on new dimensions when seen in the context of shalom. In fact, to understand them apart from shalom is at least to some extent to misunderstand the convictions about God and the world which we find at the heart of biblical faith. Seen in this perspective, we are writing an essay in biblical theology which might be called "a new look at the core of biblical faith."

This interconnectedness of the core convictions of biblical faith implies that we should make a renewed effort to place shalom more centrally in our proclamation and struggle. Placing matters relating to peace on the outer edge of faith, making them an optional, individual matter of conscience, and reducing the meaning of peace to a passive avoidance of violence have all skewed our understanding of both shalom and the central core of biblical faith. This in turn has led to the understandings and the reality described in the first part of this introduction. This essay is offered in the hope that we may begin to change these misconceptions for the good of all Christians, first world and third world, who work and struggle for the coming, at least in part, of God's kingdom.

We will begin this task with a study of the various meanings of shalom and *eirene* (the New Testament word for peace) found in the Bible. This study will form the foundation for the rest of the book. Once we are clear about the meanings of these terms, we will discuss how shalom is related to three different biblical themes—justice, salvation, and law—and how our understanding of them is changed by their connection with shalom.

Following this exploration of biblical faith, we will turn to a more historical discussion of how Israel's faith worked itself out in their national experience. The interaction of state and prophecy, especially, helps us to see more clearly what is involved in the biblical call to shalom. Jesus' ministry can then be seen as a continuation of the historical interaction of the biblical vision of shalom with other human and national aspirations. Finally, we will conclude with some implications of biblical faith for our shalom making today.

As will be readily apparent, our work here is limited in two ways. First, not all of the central convictions of biblical faith will be discussed. For example, there are no chapters on creation and history. Second, each of the chapters is far from exhaustive. They tend rather to be illustrative, pointing a direction. In the end it is not argument or evidence but conversion, transformation, and commitment that is needed. Use the following chapters as guides and stimulants for your reading and reflection on the biblical message—and your actions for peace.

In the following chapters, I have not devoted myself to giving systematic proof either that shalom is at the center of biblical faith or that the themes which I have treated are the core themes. This might be considered a lack, but I leave this to the persuasion of the material itself. What I have simply tried to do is to describe what I understand to be at least part of the central core of biblical faith. If this description and this faith make sense, both of the Bible and of your own experience, that is enough. For in the end, proof is in committing and living and seeing that, behold, all things can become new!

This discussion is offered finally in the hope that it might lead to greater clarity and understanding among people who are working for peace, both in the first world and in the third world. Shalom ought to draw all Christians together in a common struggle so that God's will might be done and God's kingdom might come on earth as it is in heaven. Above all, this essay is offered in the wish that it might enable and further the struggles for liberation of those who find themselves oppressed so that one day we might truly be brothers and sisters in God's kingdom, a kingdom which knows no first world and third world, no oppression and injustice but only shalom. But, as a first-world Christian, I am addressing myself mainly to my first-world sisters and brothers, since it is with us that the challenge of shalom for transformation must be caught in order that shalom may become a reality elsewhere.

2. Shalom: the Bible's peace

A t the entrance to McConnell Air Force Base, Wichita, Kansas, stands a large sign which says, "Peace Is Our Profession."

Others would say that war, not peace, is the work of people who have command over ICBMs poised to wipe out entire Russian cities. And President Reagan has dubbed a new MX missile system *peacekeeper*.

Clearly, the use of peace to refer to weapons intended to kill millions of civilians is opposed by those who picket military bases or who work to halt the building of nuclear arms.

Missiles: peacekeepers or threats to peace? The answer depends on how you define peace.[1] If peace has such a wide meaning that it even includes preparing for war and maintaining inequality, then everybody is for peace. But, clearly, in being for peace, everybody is not for the same thing. So we need to ask: what kind of peace?

And Christian people, who like everyone else want to be for peace, need to ask: for what kind of peace ought we work? How can we be peacemakers?

The three meanings of shalom

To answer these questions, we will search to see what the Bible aims at when it talks about peace. We shall look first at the Hebrew Bible, the Old Testament, to discover the meaning of *shalom*, the Hebrew word for peace, and then at the New Testament, the Greek Scriptures, to see the meaning of *eirene*, the Greek word for peace.

Shalom, the Hebrew word for peace, has three shades of meaning. First, it can refer to a material and physical state of affairs, this being its

---

1. This difference of definition could be seen as an argument about how to maintain or achieve peace, about means, rather than about what peace is, the end sought. But it seems to me there is here a difference in the conception of peace. What *type* of situation is being maintained by force of arms and threats of war? From observing current events, it seems evident that this power is being used to support oppression and injustice—and this is called peacekeeping! In this light, peacekeeping seems to mean maintaining a beneficial situation for some at the expense of others.

most frequent usage. It can also refer to relationships, and here it comes closest in meaning to the English word *peace*. And finally it also has a moral sense, which is its least frequent meaning.[2]

Shalom as material well-being and prosperity

Strikingly, shalom is most often used to talk about material, physical circumstances. This meaning is clear in cases where someone is asked to check on someone's shalom. In Genesis 37:14, Joseph is asked by Jacob, his father, to check on the shalom of his brothers and of the cattle. Here Jacob seems interested in knowing if they are all right physically—if they are getting along okay.

Note also Esther 2:11 and 1 Samuel 17:18. In this last reference, David is sent by his father to the army camp to see if his brothers are safe and sound. This would be a natural concern of a father whose sons are at war. In this vein, shalom can refer in a positive way to bodily good health as in Psalm 38:3.

This same sense is also found in greetings, when someone asks, "How are you?" For example, when Joseph's brothers come to the palace to see him, Joseph asks about their shalom and the shalom of their father—is he yet living? They reply that they have shalom and their father is yet living (Gen. 43:27,28).[3] In these and many similar passages (Gen. 29:6; Exod. 18:7; 2 Sam. 11:7; 18:29; 2 Kings 4:26), shalom is used to ask about the physical well-being of someone.

Informally, we might translate Joseph's question as, "Are you okay; is your father okay?" In these passages where shalom refers to the material or physical well-being of a person, it has a meaning quite different from peace as used in our speech. In fact, sometimes in reading the English text of the Bible, you would never know that the word *shalom* is being used in these passages, because it is translated *well* rather than *peace*!

Shalom is also used in the physical sense with verbs of going and

---

2. The two discussions of the meaning of shalom which I have found most helpful are: (1) C. Westermann, "Der Frieden (Shalom) im Alten Testament," in G. Picht and H. E. Todt, *Studien zur Friedensforschung* (Stuttgart: Klett, 1969), pp. 144-77. In this article, Westermann suggests *okay* as a translation for some aspects of shalom. (2) H. H. Schmid, *Shalom: Frieden im Alten Orient und im Alten Testament* (Stuttgart: KBW Verlag, 1971). Schmid particularly draws out the relationship of shalom to justice in the eighth-century prophets. Along this line, O. H. Steck, *Friedensvorstellungen im alten Jerusalem Psalmen, Jesaja, Deuterojesaja* (Zurich: Theologischer Verlag, 1972) also points to the close connection of justice and shalom.

3. If you check the references given, you will sometimes find that peace does not occur in your English translation. This is because translators do not always translate *shalom* in Hebrew by *peace* in English. This illustrates the point we are making in this chapter—shalom and peace do not have the same range of meaning.

coming, as in Jacob's prayer to God at Bethel, where he asks that he may return to his native land *in peace* (Gen. 28:21). Here we can read this as *safe and sound*. Jacob is praying that he will return safely from his flight to Mesopotamia where he is going to escape the wrath of his angry brother. (See also 2 Sam. 15:27; 19:24; 2 Chron. 15:5.)

Shalom is not only used to ask about the well-being of people, but also to ask about situations in general: "Are things all right?" or, put negatively, "Is anything the matter?" Here the inquirer wants to know if everything is as it should be. (For this type of use, see 2 Kings 5:21,22; 9:11; 2 Sam. 18:28.)

In all of these references to the material, physical realm, we can see a thread tying them together; things or people being as they ought or should be. *Shalom refers to a state of well-being, an all rightness, an okayness.*

But shalom can be even more positive than this. At some places, shalom points to more than things just being okay or all right; they're super! At these places, shalom refers to prosperity, or abundance. Indeed, the two meanings of okay and super easily shade into one another.

This usage is illustrated in the prophets' expectations for the future, where, in rosy terms, shalom depicts the changed material fortunes of Israel. See Jeremiah 33:6, 9 and Psalm 73:3 where the RSV translates shalom as *prosperity*

Because shalom has this meaning of abundance, it is also used in wishes or blessings, as in the high priestly prayer of blessing in Numbers 6:26. Here the phrase, "may God give you shalom," is a wish that the people will prosper, will meet with success in their undertakings.

This meaning is also illustrated by wishes for success. For example, in 1 Samuel 1:17, the priest Eli, after hearing Hannah's prayer, says "go in peace," a wish that she will be blessed by having her prayer granted. In these wishes for success, the desire is that affairs will be as they ought to be: ideally, people ought to succeed; failure ought not be the norm!

This meaning of shalom as prosperity, being well-off and successful, leads to its use in the context of war. Here it refers not to the opposite of war, but to success in battle! The phrase to "return in peace" from a battle often has the meaning to return victorious. This is well illustrated by 1 Kings 22:27, 28 where the prophet Micaiah has foretold defeat for the Israelite king, in fact, his death. The king responds by commanding that Micaiah be placed in prison until the king's return in shalom, that is, until he returns victorious from battle, contrary to Micaiah's prophecy. Micaiah answers by saying that if the king does indeed return from battle in shalom, victorious, then he is not a true prophet of God since he has foretold the king's defeat and death. (For other references of shalom referring to success in military matters see: Jer. 43:12, where shalom refers to Nebuchadnezzar's victory over Egypt; Isa. 41:2, of Cyrus; Judg. 8:9; 11:31.)

Finally, the word *shalom* has the negative sense of being safe and sound from some danger. Here the meaning seems to be physical security. Such use is often found in the false prophets, where they promise, as in Jeremiah 14:13, that the people will not see war, disease, or famine, but that God will give them true peace in their land. What the false prophets meant by shalom becomes clear from their opposition to Jeremiah; while Jeremiah prophesied defeat, disaster, and ruin, they promised security and a rosy future. While this use is frequent in the false prophets, it is not confined to them. (See Lev. 26:6; 1 Sam. 20:21; Job 5:24.) Part of things being as they should be is that people are safe from disasters of various kinds.

From this material meaning of shalom, which dominates in the Hebrew Bible, we need to carefully note two things. First, since in English we often use peace to refer either to relationships between people or to an inner state of mind, we must underline the fact that contrary to the English meaning of peace, shalom in the Hebrew Bible refers primarily to a physical state of well-being, to things being as they ought to be in the material world. *Shalom is marked by the presence of physical well-being and by the absence of physical threats like war, disease, and famine.*

Second, we must stress that shalom is a positive idea. It points to the *presence* of something like well-being or health, rather than having mainly a negative focus like English peace which points to the *absence* of something like war. This is important, because in English we tend to define peace as the absence of something: turmoil, distress, or war; rather than the positive presence of things as they should be. This can result in a notion that peacemakers are passive, avoiding conflict and struggle. On the contrary, shalom making is being for something—for a new situation in which people are all right with their material needs being met. *In this light, peacemaking as shalom making is striving so that those who do not now enjoy material shalom and physical well-being can do so.*

Shalom as justice

The second major realm to which shalom is linked is that of social relationships. This agrees with the way we most normally use the word *peace* in English. Shalom, like peace, can refer to positive good relations between nations or groups as in 1 Kings 5:12 or Judges 4:17. Such a peaceful relationship can be the result of a treaty as in Joshua 9:15 or Genesis 26:29,31. Like peace, shalom can be used to talk about good, regulated, normal dealings between nations. (See Num. 25:12; Ezek. 34:26; 37:26; Isa. 54:10 for God's covenant with people.)

In personal terms, shalom can be used for close friends, as in Jeremiah 20:10 where the prophet laments that even the men of his shalom, his friends, have turned against him. (See also Jer. 38:22 and Ps. 41:9.)

Negatively, shalom can be used for the opposite of war. This, as we have said, is not the primary use of shalom since it is usually a positive term pointing to the way things ought to be. But, of course, war is not the way things should be, so peace can be used to refer to the opposite of war, as well as to the opposite of disease or poverty.

While the use of shalom to talk about relationships, especially as the opposite of war, closely parallels peace in English usage, shalom's meaning extends beyond it. Just as war marked the outward absence of shalom between nations, injustice was the measure of the absence of shalom within a society.

This close tie of shalom to justice is illustrated by its use as a parallel for justice / righteousness. For example, Isaiah 60:17 is part of a description of the prophet's hope for Israel's revived fortunes in the future. The second half of this verse says:

> I will make your overseers peace
> and your taskmasters righteousness.

Verse 18 speaks of the end of internal violence and oppression. The hope is clear—when God restores the nation, Israel will practice justice. Oppression will be ended and peace will result. Isaiah 54:13-14 also contains this pairing—shalom and righteousness are signaled by the removal of oppression.

In Isaiah 32:16-17, shalom is clearly shown to be the fruit of righteousness / justice.

> Then justice will dwell in the wilderness,
>   and righteousness abide in the fruitful field
> And the effect of righteousness will be peace,
>   and the result of righteousness, quietness and trust for ever.

Literally, this passage speaks of shalom as the wages or work of righteousness.

In a different context, Psalm 35:27 also pairs righteousness with shalom. This psalm is a cry to God for deliverance from foes who threaten the petitioner. It is a plea for God to deliver one who is weak, needy, and oppressed (v. 10). At the end of the psalm, we read:

> Let those who desire my vindication [righteousness / justice]
> shout for joy and be glad,
> and say evermore,

"Great is Yahweh,
who delights in the welfare [shalom] of his servant!"

When God's deliverance comes, when justice is done, shalom results.

The expectation found in these passages that God's future revival of personal or national fortunes will result in justice and shalom is also present in passages which depict the prophets' future hope. Passages like Isaiah 9:1-7; 11:1-9 and Jeremiah 23:5-6 clearly mention the presence of justice / righteousness as a mark of the hoped for future. Also, these descriptions either mention shalom directly or describe a state which we can label shalom. Thus, in a general way, we can say that in looking forward to God's help and the restoration of their nation, the prophets expected that justice would be done, oppression removed, and shalom result.

Not only was the prophets' hope for shalom based on the doing of justice but their prediction of doom was also so based. The prophets who lived before the destruction of Jerusalem (587 B.C.E.) proclaimed disaster, not shalom. A major reason for their message of judgment was the presence of social injustice within Israel. They called both for the practice of righteousness and justice (Amos 5:21-24; Jer. 22:1-15) and condemned oppression (Jer. 22:13-17; Amos 4:1-2) which they linked directly to the coming disaster. Social injustice was, of course, not the only wrong they spoke against, but it was both frequently mentioned and clearly tied to judgment—the opposite of shalom.

Both in their estimate of the society in which they lived and in their hope for the future, the prophets saw that shalom depended on the relations among people within a society. Oppression meant no shalom, but rather judgment, while justice led to shalom.

Thus, in the arena of human relations, we see that shalom describes the way things ought to be, whether between individuals or states. Since shalom refers primarily to relations which are all right, it is not so much the absence of conflict, but the presence of positive and good relations as marked by justice. If in the material realm, shalom has the note of right being and okayness, in the relational realm, it has the note of right relatedness, of things being okay between people. This means that *shalom in the Bible involves a much wider and more positive state of affairs than a narrow understanding of peace as antiwar or antimilitary activity. Shalom making is working for just and health giving relationships between people and nations.*

Shalom as straightforwardness

Finally, the third major arena to which the word *shalom* is applied is the moral or ethical. Here we find two kinds of uses. First, shalom can be used as the opposite of deceit, as in Psalm 34:14(15), where the psalmist exhorts the seeking and pursuing of shalom, which is the opposite of speaking evil and lies. In like manner, in Psalm 37:37, I understand the phrase "man of shalom," which is paralleled by *honest*, to be the person of integrity and of straightforward character. This person is the opposite of the oppressors and the guilty of verse 38. Shalom is also used in Zechariah 8:16, where the people are told to judge with shalom, that is, with integrity.

Shalom's second moral meaning is to be blameless or innocent; without guilt. In 2 Kings 5:19, a Syrian general has been healed of his leprosy by dipping in the Jordan seven times. Because of his miraculous recovery, he wishes to worship Yahweh, the God of Israel. In order to do this, he takes some Israelite soil with him. However, he confesses to Elisha that when the king goes to worship his native god, he leans upon him for support. Thus, the general will be found in the temple aiding the worship of another god. To this Elisha replies, "Go in peace." That is to say, it's okay, you will not incur guilt.

So, in the realm of morality, shalom refers to the presence of integrity and straightforwardness, the opposite of deceit. And it is the absence of fault, guilt, or blame. In both cases, we can see again that the basic note in shalom is positive, to be the way one should be. In this sphere, we can say that *shalom making is working to remove deceit and hypocrisy and to promote honesty, integrity, and straightforwardness.*

Three meanings linked in practice

Shalom sometimes refers to material and physical conditions, sometimes to relationships, and sometimes to moral behavior. In all three of these arenas, we have traced a continuity—*shalom defines how things should be.* It describes the way people in Israelite society referred to their material world, to relationships, and to personal character which were all right.

In order to grasp how shalom relates to our situation today, it is important to keep these three aspects in mind. While it is true that sometimes one is pointed to and sometimes another, we should not choose just one part as being shalom. We ought not, for example, limit shalom to just relationships or to one kind of relationship, such as conflict or war, and forget that it includes justice as well.

In English, we use the word *healthy* in a number of ways—to speak of a person's physical as well as mental condition, for instance. Thus, when we talk about healthy persons, we sometimes mean they are all right both physically and mentally and sometimes we may mean only physically or only mentally—as when we say, "She seems to be healthy; there is nothing wrong with her physically." But just because, in this latter usage, we are only talking about physical health, we would not want to conclude that *health* means only physical health. No. We would want to say that health includes both physical and mental aspects. Likewise, with shalom: we should not limit its meaning to just one part of its range of meaning.

Furthermore, the three aspects of shalom, I believe, are linked in practice. If this is so, then all three parts need to be present to have shalom. A look at the dispute between the true and false prophets about shalom will illustrate this thesis—why it is necessary for matters to be okay materially, relationally, and morally for shalom.

While the true prophets proclaimed doom and disaster, the false prophets, more numerous and popular, told the people to expect shalom! See Jeremiah 14:10-13, and 8:11, for two examples. These passages show that the false prophets could proclaim shalom for the nation in the very situation in which the true prophets brought their message of disaster and destruction. Why?

The true prophets, seeing justice as vital for shalom, condemned social injustice and oppression. For the false prophets, on the other hand, peace seemed to mean security, avoiding the ravages of war, disease, and hunger rather than pressing for justice. We cannot say they were against justice—they probably advocated it. But evidently it was a matter of what came first and shalom for the nation did not seem to rest primarily on justice.

Why did these two groups differ on the way to achieve shalom? For the true prophets, *there could be no shalom if things were not as they ought to be*. And from their critique of society, we see that things were not all right. First, on the material level, though some people prospered—a sign of shalom as material well-being—this prosperity flourished side by side with poverty. The rich with their abundance and affluence lived in the midst of the poor and needy.

This inequality existed, secondly, because on the level of relationships, the rich and powerful were oppressing the poor and powerless. This showed that social relationships were not as they should be; oppression is not an okay relationship. And, of course, this lack of right relatedness, this oppression, led directly to material gain for some and material want for others. As a result, their prosperity only gave the outward appearance of shalom. A deeper analysis saw it for what it was, the fruit of oppression and sin (Amos 3:9-11).

Thirdly, the legal and political process was not working with honesty. As Isaiah 10:1-2 puts it, they were making unjust laws to support their own interests, with harmful results for the underclasses. The prophets complained often about bribe taking and the misuse of justice. Government guided by favoritism for special interest or classes is not government operating with integrity. Furthermore, this lack of honesty promoted oppression which destroyed hope for the material well-being for many.

Thus the argument between true and false prophets about shalom seems to boil down to whether peace / shalom refers to security and prosperity regardless of how obtained or at what price, or whether it refers to an okayness in all three aspects of life. The latter represents the true prophets' point of view.

As a result, the promise of shalom could never cover up things which were not okay. Note Ezekiel's graphic language in his harsh critique of the false prophets who said shalom when there was no shalom, thereby lulling the people with a false sense of security; as he put it, whitewashing a wall about to collapse (Ezek. 13; see verses 10 and 16 for references to shalom). Seen in this light, not all prosperity is a sign of shalom or God's grace; it may be a sign of sin and oppression calling for God's judgment. Those who mistake such a condition as peace or a time of peace surely mistake what peace is. *Only the prosperity which comes from moral integrity and includes the well-being of all is shalom prosperity.*[4] In light of this inference, we may say that <u>*justice*—not prosperity by itself—*becomes the true measuring stick for whether or not there is shalom.*</u>

This understanding of shalom has transforming meanings for our understanding of peace and peacemaking. We are tempted at times to think of peacekeeping as maintaining the status quo without conflict. But our study of shalom shows us that *peacemaking is whitewashing when we think we can have peace in spite of oppression, exploitation, and unjust laws.* To maintain a situation of oppression, material want, and deceit about the way things are is not to keep peace, but is to do the opposite! Shalom making means transforming these situations into ones of fairness, equality, and justice. *Shalom demands transformation not facade!*

Shalom as God's ultimate will

Since shalom exists where conditions are as they ought to be, it becomes a powerful symbol of God's purpose and will for our world. It is surely God's will that things be as they ought to be. We can see this in the vision of Isaiah 2:2-4. While the word *shalom* does not appear here, the scene described is shalom.

> It shall come to pass in the latter days
>   that the mountain of the house of Yahweh

---

4. There were of course other issues which separated the prophets—I have focused on the one which is germane to our discussion of shalom. However, it seems to me that notions of justice and its relationship to national security were a crucial matter distinguishing true and false prophets.

shall be established as the highest of the mountains,
  and shall be raised above the hills;
and all nations shall flow to it,
  and many peoples shall come, and say:
"Come, let us go up to the mountain of Yahweh,
  to the house of the God of Jacob;
that [God] may teach us [God's] ways
  and that we may walk in [God's] paths."
For out of Zion shall go forth the law,
  and the word of Yahweh from Jerusalem.
[God] shall judge between the nations,
  and shall decide for many peoples;
and they shall beat their swords into plowshares,
  and their spears into pruning hooks;
nation shall not lift up sword against nation,
  neither shall they learn war any more.

This picture of shalom shows the peoples recognizing the rule of God and learning the way of God, the way in which they should live. Following these two themes, the obedience of the peoples and the reign of God active in judging, shalom appears as the end result. On the one hand, shalom results when people live in obedience to God—learn God's ways and walk in them. On the other, it is also the work of God, who reigns and judges the nations.[5] When God's will is done, shalom is experienced.

Eirene, the New Testament witness

Turning to the New Testament, the word usually translated as peace is the Greek word *eirene*. It is used in much the same way as shalom—for material and physical well-being, good relationships, and moral character. We will describe these uses briefly in order to point out the continuity of meaning between shalom and eirene.

In the material realm, it is used like shalom in greetings and partings, as we can see from the openings and closings of letters. For openings see Romans 1:7; 1 Corinthians 1:3. In closings it is found in Ephesians

5. This passage also illustrates the ambiguity which often exists in terms of agency—who brings about shalom, God or people? In some passages, the emphasis is on God, as we shall see in the next chapter. In some, it is on the responsibility of people. In some, like the present passage, both God and people are active. It is fair to say, in my judgment, that there is a co-working relationship. On the one hand, we believe that God is active and wills shalom and all that it entails. On the other hand, we also believe that people are called to action as well, and that people have their task or function as well. The most powerful passage on the latter point is perhaps 2 Corinthians 5:14-21 where we are to be God's agents of reconciliation, God making appeal through us! In the end, we must hold both God's action and human responsibility together—we are co-workers with God.

6:23; 1 Peter 5:14 and 3 John 1:15. This use in letters is obviously close to the usage in wishes and blessings as in Matthew 10:13, where the disciples are to wish peace to a household in which they stay during a missionary journey. Or, again, in Mark 5:34, Jesus dismisses a woman whom he has healed with the wish of peace and health.

In relationships, eirene points to good accord, as in Acts 24:2 or Romans 14:19. Again, like shalom, eirene can also refer to the absence of conflict or war, as in Matthew 10:34, Luke 14:32, and Acts 7:26. Here we see the two poles again: on the one hand, eirene points to something positive, to the presence of good relationships; on the other hand, it can also point to the absence of proper relationships.

Finally, eirene applies to matters in the realm of the moral. Eirene is prominent as a Christian virtue. See Romans 8:6; 14:17; 15:13; Galatians 5:22; 2 Timothy 2:22; 1 Peter 3:11 and 2 Peter 3:14. Although these uses are similar to ones found for shalom, they are distinct in appearing in lists of personal virtues. Here the meaning of eirene may be closer to the English meaning of peaceable, than shalom which, as we have seen, has more to do with moral integrity.

However, eirene differs from shalom in one distinctive way: it is used theologically. That is, it is used of God as in the phrase "the God of peace," a fairly common usage in the New Testament: Romans 15:33; 16:20; 2 Corinthians 13:11; 1 Thessalonians 5:23; 2 Thessalonians 3:16; Hebrews 13:20, for example. In addition, eirene is also used in the expression "the peace of God" and "the peace of Christ," as found in John 14:27; Philippians 4:7; Colossians 3:15. We find no such phrase in the Hebrew Bible.

The New Testament also speaks of "the gospel of peace" (Eph. 6:15; also 2:17; Acts 10:36). These expressions show that in the New Testament, eirene came to have an important theological meaning: it was used to talk about God and the good news of God for humankind.

This theological significance of eirene in the New Testament comes to a peak when it is used to refer to the results of Jesus' death and resurrection. Jesus made peace in two important ways. The first is illustrated by Romans 5:1-11. In this passage, Paul begins by saying that the result of justification is peace with God; one purpose of the work of Jesus was to bring peace between people and God. This peace results from things being made right between them: justification. Paul goes on to point out that the death of Jesus which set things right was an act of God's love for helpless enemies. Thus through active enemy love and helping the helpless, God transforms divine-human relationships through Christ. There can be peace between people and God because things have been made right between them.

The result of Christ's transforming death is not only a transformation of human-divine relationships, but it also transforms affairs among people. Ephesians 2:14-17 and Colossians 1:20 refer to this effect of Christ's death. In Ephesians, it is through Christ's death that old enemies, the Jews and the Gentiles, now become one. As one body reconciled to each other, they are together reconciled to God. Here the death of Christ is shown as a transforming power among people; it sets things right between old enemies so that now there is a new positive relationship.

Note the order in Ephesians 2:14-17: first human relationships are transformed and then comes the transformation of human-divine relationships. See the same sequence also in Matthew 5:23-24. Eirene between people becomes the first step; eirene between people and God is the second.

From the point of view of these passages, can there be eirene between people and God, if there is no eirene between people? In any case, it is significant that human relations are included in the theological domain. The chief aim of life is not only finding peace with God, but also positive peace among people and classes. Lack of eirene—injustice and oppression—is not only a political and social problem, but a theological one as well. In Colossians, the vision is even grander—the whole universe will come to unity (to eirene) as a result of the work of Christ. Ecological wholeness or shalom is now included in shalom making!

Central to the New Testament is the teaching that eirene, peace as a positive concept, is central to God's purpose in Jesus Christ. Jesus came so that things might be as they ought to be both among people and between people and God and even in nature. Making things as they ought to be transforms existing relationships; new relationships take their place, relationships which are the basis for shalom.

In summing up, we have seen that eirene follows closely the meaning of shalom which we found in the Hebrew Bible. Eirene like shalom points to a positive state of affairs where things are as they should be, as God wills them to be. Within this sphere of meaning, eirene comes to have an expanded area of reference: it can also refer to things being all right or okay between God and people. *Shalom makers thus strive for total reconciliation*—among people, putting an end to want, oppression, and deception; and between people and God, so that all can live in the newness of life that is the vision of shalom. Peace / shalom seems to represent both biblical ethics and evangelism.

Making things as they ought to be

In our study of shalom and eirene, we have seen that they apply to three realms: the realm of the physical or the material, the realm of the relational or the social, and the moral sphere. In all of these areas, we have seen that the central theme is that things are as they should be, in short, all right. We have stressed that shalom and eirene usually point to something positive—they indicate the presence of the proper state of affairs. This is in contrast to peace in English which is often used as only the absence of war or conflict.

We saw in the Hebrew Scriptures a division of opinion among the prophets about whether there would be shalom. The false prophets were prophets of shalom, while the true prophets were prophets of doom. We drew from this that the false prophets were defining shalom too narrowly—as security, as the absence of disaster. The true prophets defined shalom as something which was the result of things being okay. If there was oppression and exploitation, if there was a legal system that did not redress the wrongs of the weak, and if there were the poor who were not experiencing material well-being, then things were not okay, and no amount of security could turn such a condition into shalom. *This is the central lesson of this chapter about the biblical understanding of peace—it points positively to things being as they should be; when things are not that way, no amount of security, no amount of peacekeeping in the sense of law and order and public tranquillity will make for peace.* Only a change in the way things are will allow shalom / eirene to be realized. *Only a transformation of society so that things really are all right will make for biblical peace.*

Since peace was an expression of things being as they should be, it also became the vision of how things would be when God's sovereign rule was realized. The passage in Isaiah 2:2-4 brings this to the fore. Shalom is the plan of God for human life and history, it is the sign of the coming of God's rule on earth.

In the Greek Scriptures, the use of eirene matches closely what we found for shalom, with a major exception—eirene becomes a theological term. It is used of God and Christ and of the gospel. But even more significantly, it is used to talk about the result of Christ's death. In this context, eirene refers to two aspects of human life which are to be set right by Christ's death; it transforms the relationship between people and God, and it transforms relationships between people.[6] Improper, unjust, and oppressive relationships now become a theological problem. In this we see a continuation of the hope of the prophet Isaiah—when God's sovereignty and rule is realized, shalom will be its expression.

What are the practical meanings of this for our shalom making today? It seems to me that we have tended toward too narrow a vision of what constitutes peace and peace making. Have we not tended to think of peace as either being against war or working to solve disputes between

6. This conclusion is based mainly on the material in Ephesians and Colossians cited earlier.

people, for example? If we would focus on the vision of shalom, would we not want to work so that all might enjoy an adequate material income and physical well-being? Would we not see the struggles to correct oppression as peacemaking? And would we not even see the challenge to unjust laws which work against shalom as peacemaking? In fact, would we not say that those who benefit from such a lack of shalom, but do nothing to transform the status quo, are in fact not shalom makers, but against shalom?

This leads us to several final questions. Is it not a major tragedy of the church that it has failed to fulfill either the hope of Hebrew Scriptures or the purposes of God in the atoning work of Christ for shalom? Will this not remain true until relationships within the Christian community which are now so fragmented along national and class lines are transformed? *If the coming of shalom demands a transformation, should not the church be leading the way in dismantling the structures of oppression and death wherever they are found so that shalom, God's will, may be done on earth as it is heaven?*

3. *Justice is basic*

I n the last chapter, we found that shalom and eirene refer to things being as they ought to be—being okay. Further, we saw that justice was sometimes used as a measuring stick to find out if things were okay. The dispute about shalom among the prophets made this quite clear. For the true prophets, injustice was, presumably, the opposite of shalom since it not only brought oppression but material want and deceit as well.

Given this link between justice and shalom, two questions about justice face us. What kind of justice leads to shalom? How central to biblical faith is this quest for justice and shalom?

Abraham asks God, "Shall not the judge of all the earth do what is just?" (Gen. 18:25, NEB). Here Abraham affirms a central conviction of biblical faith—God is a God for justice. Most people familiar with the Bible would agree. We would hardly expect the biblical God to be a God for injustice! What is not so clear to us from Abraham's insight, however, is the meaning of this claim for biblical faith. In relation to other parts of God's work, how basic is the concern for justice? How central for our life ought the struggle for justice become?

Doing justice is stressed by the prophets as in the familiar passage:

> "God has told you what is good;
> and what is it that Yahweh asks of you?
> Only to act justly, to love loyalty,
> to walk wisely before your God" (Micah 6:8, NEB).

This passages points to the importance of doing justice—it is a basic concern of those who follow the God of justice. However, the prophet does not tell us how we are to put it into practice in the world today. What does it mean to act justly according to the Bible?

Indeed, since the rise of liberation theology and our awareness of worldwide hunger and poverty, this question has increased urgency. What is biblical justice and how can we get it? This has become a major, if not *the* major, concern for Christian people today.

In order to gain a background from which we can answer these questions, we need to find out just how important justice is in the Bible's picture of who God is. Second, we will try to define God's justice and show how this justice aims at and leads to shalom.[1]

Justice is basic to God's rule

We will base our study of God's connection with justice on the psalms because they express clear and heartfelt sentiments about why the God of Israel is to be worshiped. One of the reasons given is because this God works for justice. For example, Psalm 89:5-14:

> Let the heavens praise thy wonders, O Yahweh,
>> thy faithfulness in the assembly of the holy ones!
> For who in the skies can be compared to Yahweh?
>> Who among the heavenly beings is like Yahweh,
> a God feared in the council of the holy ones,
>> great and terrible above all that are round about him?
> O Yahweh God of hosts,
>> who is mighty as thou art, O Yahweh,
>> with thy faithfulness round about thee?
> Thou dost rule the raging of the sea [*Yam*];
>> when its waves rise, thou stillest them
> Thou didst crush Rahab like a carcass,
>> thou didst scatter thy enemies with thy mighty arm.
> The heavens are thine, the earth also is thine;
>> the world and all that is in it, thou hast founded them.
> The north and the south, thou hast created them;
>> Tabor and Hermon joyously praise thy name.
> Thou hast a mighty arm;
>> strong is thy hand, high thy right hand.
> Righteousness and justice are the foundation of thy throne;
>> steadfast love and faithfulness go before thee.

This passage asks, Who or what other god is as great as Yahweh, the God of Israel? There may be other gods or divine beings, but none of them can compare to Israel's God. Why? Because Yahweh is the Creator God. God's act of creation is shown here through poetic battle images in which Yahweh defeats the dragons and monsters (sea, Yam, and

---

1. On the theme of biblical justice, I have found the following two sources helpful, among many others: H. H. Schmid, *Gerechtigkeit als Weltordnung. Hintergrund und Geschichte des alttestamentlichen Gerechtigkeitsbegriffs* (Tubingen, 1968) and J. Miranda, "Law and Civilization," in *Marx and the Bible* (Orbis), pp. 109-99.

Rahab). This battle imagery was also used by Israel's neighbors. For example, in *Enuma Elish*, a Babylonian epic poem, it is Marduk, the god of Babylon, who subdues the monsters. Following his conquest, Marduk creates, with the help of other gods, heaven and earth. Thereupon, he is proclaimed king by the gods.

In this psalm, however, the motif of battle is used to argue for the majesty of Israel's God above all other gods because it was Yahweh alone who subdued the dragons and monsters and created the universe. First, then, God's unique majesty and lordship is based upon creation.

Following this affirmation comes the further claim that righteousness and justice are the foundation of this God's throne. That is to say, justice is the basis for the rule and kingship of God over the universe just created. Doing justice is the foundation of God's rule.

These two claims, that God is creator and that God rules through doing justice, form the joint basis in the psalm for the belief that no other god or divine being can rival the greatness of Israel's God. As a result, it is Yahweh who is to be worshiped and praised.

From this psalm, we learn that while God's act of creation gave God the right to be the sovereign of the universe, it is justice which describes God's kingship. Or, put another way, we might say that it is creation which showed God's power to be sovereign; but it is God's use of justice which gives God the right to be the king of Israel.

Psalm 33 also links justice to God's act of creation. In the first three verses, the congregation is invited to praise God. Then come the reasons why:

> [God] loves righteousness and justice;
> the earth is full of the steadfast love of Yahweh (v. 5).

Following this mention of justice and righteousness, verses 6-9 mention creation, while 10-22, the bulk of the psalm, portray God's rule in history. Again we see the Creator God who is sovereign relating to the world through the rule of justice.

In these two examples, God as a God of justice is connected with God as the creator of the world. But elsewhere in the psalms, God is spoken of as ruler or king without mention of creation. In these cases, too, justice is presented as basic to God's action. For example, Psalm 9:7, 8, where judging is seen as a royal exercise of authority:

> But Yahweh sits enthroned for ever,
> [God] has established his throne for judgment;
> and [God] judges the world with righteousness,
> [God] judges the peoples with equity (vv. 7, 8).

(See also Ps. 99:1-4 and 96:10-13.)

From these confessions about God, it seems clear that, for biblical faith, God's rule of the world and the exercise of justice go hand in hand. *Justice expresses the primary characteristic of God's action in the world and its history.*

Justice is basic to God being God

But the linking of God and justice means more than Yahweh's right to rule and the use of God's royal power to gain justice. The very claim that Yahweh, the God of Israel, is *divine* rather than the supposed gods of the nations, rests on Yahweh's deeds of justice. This is strikingly shown in Psalm 82, where the God of Israel takes a stand in the council of the gods.

> God has taken his place in the divine council;
>   in the midst of the gods he holds judgment:
> "How long will you judge unjustly
>   and show partiality to the wicked? *Selah*
> Give justice to the weak and the fatherless;
>   maintain the right of the afflicted and the destitute.
> Rescue the weak and the needy;
>   deliver them from the hand of the wicked" (vv. 1-4).

In this speech, God accuses the gods of the nations because, rather than upholding justice, they corrupt it. Rather than aiding those in need, they, in fact, assist those doing injustice. The abuse of justice carried on by the other gods leads to the following conclusion:

> They have neither knowledge nor understanding,
>   they walk about in darkness;
> all the foundations of the earth are shaken (v. 5).

Their failure to pursue justice shows that the other gods are ignorant and therefore poor guides; they walk about in darkness. Furthermore, as a result of their failure to practice justice, the created order itself is affected. This reflection on the ignorance of the gods and the harmful outcome of their actions on earth leads the psalmist to a further conclusion:

> I [used to(?)] say, "You are gods,
>   sons of the Most High, all of you;
> nevertheless, you shall die like men,
>   and fall like any prince."

Arise, O God, judge the earth;
for to thee belong all the nations! (vv. 6-8).

The other gods are in fact no gods. The God of Israel alone is the true God because only the God of Israel brings justice to the weak and oppressed. Since Yahweh alone promotes justice, Israel's God alone is the ruler of all nations.

This argument is based on the conviction that since justice is part of the rightful exercise of kingship, only a god who is a god of justice can really be God—because only such a being can truly rule and exercise power. Justice becomes *the* quality that defines what it means for God to be God. A god without the exercise of justice is no god at all.

Similar sentiments are found in Psalm 58:1-2:

Do you indeed decree what is right, you gods?
Do you judge the sons of men uprightly?
Nay, in your hearts you devise wrongs;
your hands deal out violence on earth.

Do the gods really do justice? The psalmist says no. They plot and do violence instead. The psalm ends with a plea for the true God to bring about justice, because when evildoers are judged, people say, "Surely there is a God who judges [rules] on earth" (v. 11). One's faith in God goes hand in hand with God doing justice.

We now have an answer for one of the questions with which we began this chapter: *for biblical faith, the doing of justice was essential to the nature and being of God and for the actions and purposes of God on earth in history.* We can now raise the second question: What type of justice is basic for biblical faith?

God's justice

Earlier, we quoted Abraham's question, "Will not the Lord of all the earth do right?" Abraham's concern that the sovereign Lord must act justly is not surprising to us. Justice is one of those virtues which we prize highly; we would expect God to display it in a perfect manner. But we also know from experience that standards and ideas about what is just and how justice is done differ. This means that when we say that the Bible portrays God as a God of justice, we must go on to ask: What kind of justice is linked to God? What acts of justice form the foundation for God's rule over the world? To get at this question, we will begin by asking how God isportrayed as a God of justice in the psalms.

We begin with the psalms again because in them we see God's justice in a strikingly clear way. Many psalms represent the cry of those who feel justice has been and is being denied them.[2] Let's look at several of these psalms in order to see how they describe God's justice.

The theme of God doing justice is often linked in the psalms with a plea for God's deliverance from enemies who are acting harmfully toward the one who is praying. Psalm 9 is a good example of this motif.

> When my enemies turned back,
>   they stumbled and perished before thee.
> For thou hast maintained my just cause;
>   thou hast sat on the throne giving righteous judgment
> (vv. 3-4).

God, as a judge or ruler, *delivers* the one who is threatened. For the psalmist, this personal experience of God's delivering justice leads, in the following verses, to a broader affirmation about God. God's justice is not only experienced on the personal level but on the national level as well.

But what does this just rule mean for those on earth? How can it be stated more clearly? The answer comes in later verses.

> The wicked shall depart to Sheol,
>   all the nations that forget God.
> For the needy shall not always be forgotten,
>   and the hope of the poor shall not perish for ever.
> Arise, O Yahweh! Let not man prevail;
>   let the nations be judged before thee!
> Put them in fear, O Yahweh!
>   Let the nations know that they are but men! (vv. 17-20).

God's universal judgment of the nations is a judgment against the powerful and for the helpless, the needy, and the poor. From this psalm, the first point we may make about God's justice is that it delivers the needy. The second is its counterpoint: God's justice is against the powerful. It places them in fear, it puts them in their place, restraining them. A justice which benefits the weak and oppressed and moves against the powerful is what God's rule of the world is like.

The understanding of God's justice as aid for the weak, the poor, and oppressed, and breaking the power of the oppressor is expressed again in Psalm 10. It begins with a complaint and a plea.

---

2. Laments make up about one half of the Book of Psalms. They are prayers representing the reaching out for God by those in despair because they feel the injustices of life and the absence of God.

Why dost thou stand afar off, O Yahweh?
Why dost thou hide thyself in times of trouble?
In arrogance the wicked hotly pursue the poor;
let them be caught in the schemes which they have devised
(vv.1-2).

Here we are told that it is the wicked who oppress the poor. The psalm ends with a plea for God to act, since, as the writer points out, God is the hope of justice for the weak and needy:

Break thou the arm of the wicked and evildoer;
seek out his wickedness till thou find none.
Yahweh is king for ever and ever;
the nations shall perish from his land.
O Yahweh, thou wilt hear the desire of the meek;
thou wilt strengthen their heart, thou wilt incline thy ear
to do justice to the fatherless and the oppressed,
so that man who is of the earth may strike terror no more
(vv. 15-18).

Again, God's rule as king of the universe is firmly marked by a justice which deals with the plight of the weak and the oppressed in two ways. First, it brings judgment on the oppressors—here expressed as breaking their arm—their power so that they "may strike terror no longer." Second, the oppressed are delivered.

Before going on, it is worth noticing the middle part of this psalm (10:3-14). Here the wicked who are oppressing the weak are described. This sketch ends with the innermost thoughts of the oppressor: he oppresses because he does not think God makes any difference—God does not take note of what happens on the earth, so the strong might as well take advantage of the weak!

He says to himself, "God has forgotten;
he has hidden his face and has seen nothing" (v. 11, author's translation).

We call this attitude of the oppressor practical atheism, living as if God doesn't make any real difference in life. Here practical atheism shows itself through oppression. If God did make a difference for them, they would not oppress. *Since God's rule is shown through a liberating justice for the oppressed, oppression is a mark of atheism.*

Other psalms could be cited which also link God's rule with a justice expressed as deliverance and aid for the weak and oppressed (68:6-7; 76:9; 103:6; 109:31; 113:5-9; 140:12-13), but I will cite just one final example, Psalm 146, which spells out this conviction at some length.

This psalm begins with a warning to trust in God only. Then two grounds are given for praising the God of Jacob; first, because this is the God who made heaven and earth. Then, second, without pausing, the psalm continues on into history, how the sovereign God is now at work:

> who keeps faith for ever;
>> who executes justice for the oppressed;
>> who gives food to the hungry.
> Yahweh sets the prisoners free;
>> Yahweh opens the eyes of the blind.
> Yahweh lifts up those who are bowed down;
>> Yahweh loves the righteous.
> Yahweh watches over the sojourners,
>> he upholds the widow and the fatherless;
>> but the way of the wicked he brings to ruin.
> Yahweh will reign for ever,
>> thy God, O Zion, to all generations (vv. 6-10).

As in the psalms mentioned above, and especially Psalm 82, God's justice is shown in a positive way by care for those who are weak and oppressed: prisoners, blind, bowed down, aliens, widows, and fatherless. These persons are the objects of God's positive justice. On the other side of this justice coin, God's justice punishes those who oppress the needy: God brings the way of the wicked to ruin.

Justice as fortunes reversed

This conviction that God's justice is a transforming power directed toward the plight of the powerless is expressed even where the words *justice* or *righteousness* are not used. It is reflected, for example, in passages in which God's concern for the underdog, the little ones at the bottom of the heap, is shown through a reversal of fortunes; the poor are lifted up and the powerful are brought down. The psalm of Hannah (1 Sam. 2:1-10) depicts this theme; the feeble will get strength, the hungry will find food, the lowly will be raised, and the barren will bear children. On the opposite side, the weapons of the mighty are broken and the overfed become hirelings. (See also Ps. 113 where reversal of fortunes is tied into God's universal kingship.)

This theme also appears in key places in the New Testament, for example, in Luke 1:46-55. This is Mary's song, the Magnificat, uttered in praise of the coming birth and ministry of Jesus. In this poem, Mary extols the majesty of God, a greatness marked by the following acts:

[God] has scattered the proud in the imagination of their hearts,
[God] has put down the mighty from their thrones,
and exalted those of low degree;
[God] has filled the hungry with good things,
and the rich he has sent empty away (vv. 51-53).

The reversal of fortunes motif, as part of God's work for justice, highlights God's justice as aid and deliverance for those in need. The childless have children, the lowly are exalted, the poor are poor no longer, while the power of the mighty is broken; the rulers have come down off their thrones. *When God's justice is done, the situation of inequity is transformed.*

Mary's song was given by way of hope for the work of the one she was to bear. Jesus did not disappoint the hope expressed here; the theme of reversed fortunes comes through powerfully in his ministry. One of the clearest examples is the Beatitudes in Luke 6:20-26:

And he lifted up his eyes on his disciples, and said:
"Blessed are you poor, for yours is the kingdom of God.
"Blessed are you that hunger now, for you shall be satisfied.
"Blessed are you that weep now, for you shall laugh.
"Blessed are you when men hate you, and when they exclude you and revile you, and cast out your name as evil, on account of the Son of man! Rejoice in that day, and leap for joy, for behold, your reward is great in heaven; for so their fathers did to the prophets.
"But woe to you that are rich, for you have received your consolation.
"Woe to you that are full now, for you shall hunger.
"Woe to you that laugh now, for you shall mourn and weep.
"Woe to you, when all men speak well of you, for so their fathers did to the false prophets."

These blessings and woes vividly describe the reversal of fortunes which God's justice will bring about. The powerful and wealthy will not continue in their present state of prosperity; the needy will have their needs met.[3]

Justice as vindication

God's justice as aid for those in need, the weak and oppressed, explains what appears to be a strange fact in the psalms as well as elsewhere in

---

3. The book by Don Kraybill, *The Upside Down Kingdom* (Herald Press, 1978) elaborates this theme of Jesus' teaching in Luke.

the Bible: when suffering persons pray to God for justice, they often pray for God to judge them according to God's justice. We might think this a risky prayer. What if God judges and they are found guilty? Better to leave well enough alone! The apparent strangeness and riskiness of this prayer vanishes when we realize that God's justice is not thought of as the way of arriving at a decision pronouncing someone guilty or innocent. *Rather, God's justice is an act which aids those in distress.*

Given this conviction, we can see the sense in a plea for judgment by those who are poor, weak, or oppressed. They are not asking for a trial, but for help since God's justice meant deliverance for them. This is why the plea "judge me" which occurs at the beginning of some psalms, like 26 and 43, is translated in the RSV as "vindicate me." The justice of God vindicates those in need by delivering them from the powerful and the oppressors.

God's justice defined

To sum up this material, we can say that God's justice is characterized in two basic ways. First, God is judge of all the nations, the whole earth (Ps. 9:7-8; 9:20; 67:4; 82:8; 94:2; 96:13). This we might describe as the range of God's justice, its quantity.

Second, this universal justice expresses itself through acts on behalf of the underclass who gain relief and liberation through the exercise of justice (Ps. 7:11; 9:8; 10:18; 37:9; 76:10; 103:6; 140:13; 146:7). We might label this the quality of God's justice.

We return now to the question with which we began: what is the nature of God's justice? what are the marks of God's justice? Two things seem obvious. First, in terms of its object, God's justice is shown to the poor, the disadvantaged, and the weak. This was seen not only in the persons named as objects of God's justice, but also in the reversal of fortunes theme and in the plight of those praying for God's justice.

Second, in terms of its results, God's justice helps the needy, it delivers people from bad circumstances, whether it be hunger, prison, or another case of suffering or form of oppression. *God's justice sets things right, it is a liberating justice.*

God's justice which sets things right takes two forms. First, God's justice delivers the underclass from their oppression and transforms their situation. Second, God's justice judges the oppressors; it shatters the power which enables them to oppress. In the psalms quoted above, oppressive power opposes God's rule—it is a sign of atheism, it is sin. In short, *God's justice as shown and sought in the psalms demolishes the oppressive status quo by acting for the disadvantaged and oppressed, and by crushing their oppressors.*

Since material want, oppression, and lack of moral integrity are the opposites of shalom, God's acts of justice reverse a non-shalom situation. God's justice makes things right by transforming the status quo of need and oppression into a situation where things are as they should be. This transformation forms the basis for shalom. Given this connection between God's justice and shalom, we shall call this shalom justice. And where shalom justice is missing, there shalom is missing. *Peacemaking means working for the realization of shalom justice which is necessary for the realization of shalom.*

Flowing from these two aspects of God's justice—the object (the underclass and needy) and the objective (shalom)—is another major characteristic of God's justice, perhaps its most basic aspect: *God's action for justice is not based on the merit of individuals, but on their need.* The fact of their oppression calls forth from God an act of justice. The fact that they are blind makes them an object of God's care. Nothing in Psalm 146, quoted above, says that it was some special merit on the part of the needy that caused God to act for them. Shalom justice is not based on calculating what people deserve, but rather on making an unright situation a right one. *God's justice is a response to the lack of shalom in order to create the conditions of shalom.*

An illustration of this principle is found in John 9. Jesus and his disciples come across a blind man. The disciples ask, "Who is to blame [who sinned], this man or his parents?" Jesus answered: "It was not that this man sinned, or his parents, but that the works of God might be made manifest in him. We must work the works of him who sent me, while it is day; night comes, when no one can work" (vv. 3, 4).

Jesus' answer implies that placing blame is not the point, nor fixing responsibility. Rather this situation of need is an opportunity to work the work of God—to transform the situation by curing this man from his blindness. While we are prone to assess blame—the plight of the poor and disadvantaged is their own fault—or to assign responsibility—someone else is responsible for their situation—Jesus acts to deal with the need. He performs an act of shalom justice. Regardless of all other considerations, people ought to see rather than to be blind! People ought to be liberated rather than be oppressed. As a result, *shalom makers are more concerned with transforming situations rather than meting out what people deserve.*

God's justice versus human standards

We can sharpen our understanding of shalom justice by comparing it with our normal notions of justice. Usually, we understand it as being either retributive or distributive.

Retributive justice measures out punishment. If someone does something wrong, retributive justice decrees that they suffer for their misdeed. Our criminal law is based on this kind of justice, for example. The aim of this type of justice is not to set things right, but to punish, making sure people get what is coming to them for their misdeeds. This is illustrated, for instance, by the fact that victims of crime receive no compensation for injuries or damages. Retributive justice does not aim to set things right with the victims.

Because God often does not operate according to retributive justice, sometimes complaints are raised against God. An example is found in the Book of Jonah. After a false start and a fishy detour, Jonah ends up proclaiming that in forty days, the city of Nineveh will be destroyed. Following this, Jonah retires to a place outside the city to see the fireworks. However, much to his dismay, God does not destroy the city. The people repented after hearing Jonah's message and as a result God decided not to destroy the city. This, of course, was just what Jonah feared and was the reason he did not want to go and speak God's message in the first place. Jonah wanted to see retributive justice carried out, but that was not the justice of God.

Now, to be sure, we do find cases of God's wrath and vengeance. But to understand this side of God's justice, we need to see it in context. Shalom justice has two sides: aid for the needy is one; the other is the breaking of the power of the oppressor. For without judgment on the oppressor, how can the oppressed be freed? The wrath of God expresses the judgment of God against those who are oppressors, those who support an unjust status quo of no shalom.[4]

The vengeance of God is also linked to shalom justice in prayers for God's aid. The plea for God's vindication, as Moshe Greenberg points out, is a plea for God to act when there is no chance of obtaining justice by process.[5] Here again God acts retributively but with a view to bring shalom justice to those who are unable to obtain it within the status quo. The example of Samson, concerning whom Greenberg makes these remarks, illustrates the cry for God's vengeance by someone who has no hope of gaining justice / liberation from his oppressors. Samson cries to God to meet his need, to avenge him on his enemies. God listens to his prayer and gives him the opportunity to act on his own behalf against his tormentors.

So, then, Scripture does contain the notion of God's retributive justice. But, as in the examples above, it is often to be understood within the context of God's shalom justice. For it results both in the punishment of those who maintain an unjust situation and in the re-

---

4. For a treatment of God's punishing righteousness from a New Testament perspective see, John Piper, "The Demonstration of the Righteousness of God in Romans 3:25,26," *Journal for the Study of the New Testament* 7(1980)2-32; and ibid., "The Righteousness of God in Romans 3:1-8," *Theologische Zeitschrift* 36(1980)3-16.

5. Moshe Greenberg, *Biblical Prose Prayer as a Window to the Popular Religion of Ancient Israel* (Berkeley: University of California Press, 1983), p. 13.

dressing of the wrongs of those who cannot obtain justice because of their powerlessness. As a result, *shalom makers working for shalom justice will not only work with the poor and oppressed to change their situation, but they will also struggle against the oppressors in order to break the grip of their oppression. Shalom justice demands a double struggle!*[6]

Making retribution serve the goal of shalom both tempers and limits the practice of retributive justice. Unfortunately, such an aim is not always, or perhaps even usually, the case in our modern practice of justice. Often it is those who need shalom justice—the poor, the oppressed, the underclass—who are punished.

An example of this in my experience was the appointment of crime busters by the government of the Philippines in spring of 1985. These plainclothesmen were authorized to shoot on sight. This was the government's response to a worsening economic situation in which the poor were driven to desperate measures to keep themselves and their families alive. While the poor were being gunned down in Manila, the ruling elite, according to news reports, were hiding billions of dollars abroad, making the economic situation even worse. Thus, retributive justice becomes a way the powerful and advantaged use to punish the powerless and needy. Too often, rather than setting things right and making shalom, we punish.

Distributive justice

The second major way in which we think of justice is termed distributive justice. This notion of justice has to do with what we consider to be a fair distribution of rewards, material goods, and prestige. We generally hold that people should be rewarded according to merit, according to what they deserve on the basis of what they have earned. Again, distributive justice has a place. We find it in the Bible and it has its place today. People ought to reap the fruits of their labor.

But it is also true that some sow and do not reap, while others who have not sown, do reap. Furthermore, not all can sow or reap because not all have access to means for producing a livelihood for themselves. That is, what we consider merit is not equally distributed. Some people have a better chance to gain the goods society has to offer.

For example, some, by reason of birth, come to control large capital resources such as factories or farms. Others have better educational and occupational chances. These persons, by our standards, are held to

---

6. This is not to say that God's retributive justice falls only on oppressors; it also falls on other manifestations of rebellion against God as well. What we want to stress is that, in the context of shalom justice, it does have a positive purpose, not just the punishment of the wrongdoer.

merit the prosperity and power which they obtain, while those not as fortunate or hardworking are held to have little merit and, as a result, their poverty is justified. In the case of unequal access to resources and opportunities, distributive justice can become an excuse for unequal distribution. It justifies wealth and poverty existing side by side. This inequality leads to the need for shalom justice: changes in the situation so that the powerless and needy can meet their needs.

We can say that our usual notions of justice are based on the idea of reciprocity, of tit for tat. This is true both of punishments (retributive justice) and of rewards (distributive justice). This tit for tat justice does have its proper place. However, the problem arises when reciprocity is not tempered by shalom justice and as a result it operates to maintain the status quo, preserving the rights of those who have against the needs of those who have not.

From this glance at our normal ways of thinking about justice, we can see why the poor, the needy, and the oppressed are the Bible's litmus test for whether or not justice is being done. It is exactly this underclass which is not well served by reciprocity systems of justice. As mentioned above, retribution is used to keep them down. Distributive justice passes them by.

As a result, in our notions of justice, the aim becomes not to bring shalom, but to preserve the status quo—law and order. Law then functions to preserve our security and our position, not as something which transforms society and brings about social justice. In contrast, shalom justice operates according to need regardless of merit; first, it takes seriously the needs of those who do not have. In so doing, biblical justice aims at creating shalom, because *only a justice which is based on need will really serve the interest of the underclass and transform their situation from one of need and oppression to one of sufficiency and freedom. Shalom demands that peacemakers work for this justice if shalom is to become a reality.*

Toward structures more just

We now understand how important justice is to biblical faith. From our study of several psalms, we found that it is basic: the rule of God is founded on justice. Furthermore, it is the promotion of justice which distinguishes the true God from the false gods. Justice action is basic to God being God!

Second, we tried to define the nature of God's justice: what is the quality of God's action and rule in the world? Again, we looked at several psalms. In these we found the central conviction that God's justice is seen in action for the needy, the powerless, and oppressed. God's justice was shown in the meeting of their needs and the transforming of their situation through aid and liberation.

This led us to characterize God's justice as shalom justice, a justice which, based on need, aims to transform in order that things might be okay. We contrasted this justice with our usual understanding of justice as retributive or distributive. These, we saw, are based on the notion of reciprocity—giving to people according to our judgment of what they deserve—rather than aiding them according to their need. Since such justice often preserves the status quo, it does not set things right and may, through preserving an oppressive situation, actually hinder the realization of shalom. Only justice which liberates and transforms will bear shalom.

It would seem then that those who acknowledge the God of the Bible would be concerned to create and support systems of justice which echo God's justice rather than those which thwart it. Furthermore, from both the commands in the Bible to do justice (See the Micah passage quoted at the beginning of this chapter.) and the work of people doing shalom justice, it seems evident that such work is a vital task for the people of God. We will reinforce this point in the chapters on Law, which is about doing justice, and on the state which is to be the means for justice.

Given these findings, why have the church and Christian people been so active in charity—distributing excess—but relatively inactive in changing the structures which allow need and make charity necessary? Why have we been more concerned with giving aid which leaves injustice and oppression untouched than with developing just structures? Does not shalom making require meeting the needs of the powerless and their liberation from the oppression which causes their need? It would seem that *peacemakers must struggle against oppressors and oppressive structures, since until their power is broken, the needy and oppressed cannot go free and there can be no shalom.*

The other half of the struggle, of course, requires us to erect more just structures and systems in which shalom can be experienced. This positive task will be difficult, but our struggle for justice must be carried on with a sense of humility and dependence on the God of justice.

4. Salvation: shalom justice in action

I srael believed its God alone was the god who practiced justice. Justice was the foundation of God's kingship and rule over the world. Doing justice was basic to God being God.

In probing the quality of God's justice, we discovered it to be based on need rather than merit. It was a justice aimed at meeting the needs of the weak, the poor, and the oppressed. We called this shalom justice because it transformed conditions of need and oppression into ones where things were okay, and where shalom could be found.

Now, we want to take the next step and ask: What led the people of Israel to make this claim about their God? Where did Israel see or experience God at work in the world in this way? Where did they experience God bringing about shalom justice?

Let's reflect on how God was experienced in the Bible. If we were to sum up how God was at work in history, I believe we would say *salvation* since, in the Bible, salvation is central to what God is about. Indeed, many regard salvation as more important to the Bible than justice because, after all, the Bible is, in part, a history of God's saving acts. This theme is also affirmed by the mission of the church today— proclaiming God's salvation. God, the church says, is still a God who saves.

Since, according to the psalms, God's rule in the world is marked by justice, we can expect God's work of salvation to also be flavored by justice. For example, in Psalm 105, beginning with verse 5, God's actions and justice are linked together. The psalm relates Israel's history by focusing on God saving Israel from Egypt. This salvation event gives content and context to the psalm's claim that God's justice extends over the whole earth—even over Egypt. So, we are led to ask: Does experience of salvation form a basis for understanding God as a God for shalom justice?

God's salvation is most centrally illustrated by two great acts: the salvation of the Israelites from Egypt, just mentioned, and the salvation through Jesus. These are the two foundation events, the former for the Hebrew Scriptures and Jewish people, the latter for the Greek Scriptures and Christian people. These two acts are basic because they provide us with models of salvation that define the nature and character of God's salvation. In this chapter, we will examine the Exodus and the general understanding of salvation as we find it in the Bible. In the next chapter, we will consider Jesus' death and atonement.

Exodus: God's founding act of salvation

It is widely recognized that the exodus of Israel from Egypt was the founding fact of Israel's existence. It was also the most significant event in its understanding of God. As such, it lies at the base of Israel's faith. How did Israel understand this primary event?

It seems clear from the story itself that Israel's deliverance was due to its need, its oppression, and its cry to God which was heard. The story begins in Exodus 2:23-25:

> Years passed, and the king of Egypt died, but the Israelites still groaned in slavery. They cried out, and their appeal for rescue from their slavery rose up to God. [God] heard their groaning, and remembered [the] covenant with Abraham, Isaac, and Jacob; [God] saw the plight of Israel, and he took heed of it (NEB).

The story continues with an account of the action God took in response to this cry for deliverance. God called Moses from the burning bush, asking him to return to Egypt and help deliver the people, for God said,

> I have seen the affliction of my people . . . their cry because of their taskmasters. . . . I have come down to deliver [save] them out of the hand of the Egyptians . . . the cry of the people of Israel has come to me, and I have seen the oppression with which the Egyptians oppress them. Come, I will send you (3:7-10).

Several points should be noted from this account. First is the notion that the Exodus was an act of salvation. Although the Hebrew words describing God's actions are translated in various ways, these are the words Israel used to talk about God's saving action. I have tried to show this in the above quotation by the use of square brackets.

Second, we can see that God's act of salvation is based on Israel's oppression. Since this act of salvation met the people's need for freedom from oppression, this act can also be understood as an act of shalom justice. Thus, salvation from Egypt, since it liberated the powerless from oppression, is a good example of what the psalms describe as God's justice. We can say, for the time being, that *God's salvation of*

Israel from slavery is an expression of God's justice; it helped those in need, corrected injustice and thus brought shalom.

Salvation in the Hebrew Scriptures

This finding that God's salvation is the sign of shalom justice needs to be tested more widely. How did the people of Israel understand God's salvation? Did they usually think of it, as in the Exodus, as liberation from oppression and need?

To answer this question, we will study some of the key words which Israel used to talk about salvation. From this broader base, we can see whether God's salvation of Israel from Egypt is unique, or whether this is generally how God's salvation was understood.

We begin our word study with a look at the way the word *hoshia* is used in the Bible. This verb, often translated *to save*, is the most common word used to describe God's saving acts in the Hebrew Bible.

First, we should note that this verb is also used with humans as its subject. For example, in Exodus 2:17, we read, "The shepherds came and drove them away; but Moses stood up and helped [literally, *saved*] them, and watered their flock." Here Moses is the subject of the word *save*. His act of salvation was helping the daughters of Reuel water their father's flock since they were being kept back by the more powerful male shepherds.

This word is also applied to men who act as agents of God in saving their people. In the Book of Judges, many of the men who save Israel from their oppressors are called *saviors* or are said to *save* Israel. (See Judg. 3:9, 15, 31; 6:14, 36; 10:1; 13:5, for example.) Often the word *hoshia* will not be translated *save* in English, but *deliver*. In these cases, it is clear that *hoshia* is being used to express Israel's liberation from the oppression of other nations. This use clearly parallels God's action in delivering Israel from Egypt.

However, as suggested above, the word is often used of God. If we look at the cases where God is the subject of the verb and ask how God's saving action is shown and from what God saves people, we find the following:

God is often said to save people from their enemies, from nations who are oppressing them. Examples of this would be Exodus 14:30 where God saves Israel from the Egyptian army which was pursuing them in order to return them to slavery. Or, again, in Judges 7:7, God promises to save Israel from the Midianites; or in 1 Samuel 14:23, God saves Israel from the Philistines.

Now, besides saving people from their national and political enemies, God saves people from their personal distresses. Psalm 34:6 says, "This poor man cried, and Yahweh heard him, and saved him out of all his troubles." Because God acts to deliver the poor and oppressed from their misery, we find, in Jeremiah 14:8, the people praying, "O thou hope of Israel, its savior in time of trouble." In time of drought, the people are praying for a return of fertility to the land. They believe that God is a God who saves those who are in trouble, those who find themselves at the mercy of others or natural forces.

What is quite striking is that while *hoshia* is used of God saving people from material and physical oppression, it is almost never used of God saving people from moral defects or problems. Only in two late references is it applied to the moral realm. In Ezekiel 36:29, it is promised that, in the future, God will save the people from their uncleanness; while in Ezekiel 37:23, God will save them from their backsliding. It is striking that *hoshia* is never used in Hebrew Scriptures with sin as the object from which people are saved!

The same pattern is seen in the case of the noun, *yesh'ua*, salvation, which comes from the verb *hoshia*. It is used of God in Exodus 14:13 and 15:2 with reference to the salvation of Israel from Egypt. It also is used of God's salvation of people from oppression and oppressors, as in Psalm 3:2, 8; 13:5. It is never used of God's salvation from spiritual or moral defects like sin.

From this, we conclude that in Hebrew Scriptures salvation was primarily a political, material term since *save* refers to the liberation of people from physical and political oppression and from conditions of material distress like droughts and famine. Thus a better translation of *hoshia* into English would be liberation. *Salvation is liberation!*

Unlike English, where we can use *save* to refer to saving money or things, *hoshia* is only used of saving people. This may imply that the term has less of a meaning of conserving or preserving than does save in English. God's salvation is not aimed at conserving the status quo but at transforming it by liberating those who are oppressed!

This study of *hoshia* is so striking, so at odds with our normal understanding of God's salvation, that our first impulse is to think that something has gone wrong. However, when we explore other words used to refer to God's saving action, we get much the same result. For example, *hassil* like *hoshia* is used to describe God saving people from their foes, like the Egyptians in Exodus 3:8; 12:27; 18:9,10, or from the Philistines in 1 Samuel 7:3,14. It is used to sum up Israel's cry for God's salvation from their enemies in 1 Samuel 12:10,11. Again, in these references, as in the case of *hoshia*, the RSV often translates the word by *deliverance* rather than *salvation* or *save*.

Hassil, like *hoshia*, is also used to speak of God's salvation of the individual from physical peril. In 1 Samuel 26:24, David hopes that just as he has been merciful to Saul, sparing his life when he could have killed him, so may God "deliver [*hassil*] me out of all tribulation." Or again in Psalm 54, a prayer begins with a request for God's justice to be done, for God to vindicate. (See our previous chapter for justice as vindication of the oppressed, pages 28-31.) The psalm ends with an expression of gratitude: "For thou hast delivered [*hassil*] me from every trouble, and my eye has looked in triumph on my enemies." As in the case of *hoshia*, God's saving action is almost always seen in material and political terms. God's salvation meant political liberation from national enemies or from personal foes.

Also, like *hoshia*, *hassil* is used only twice with spiritual meaning. In Psalm 39:8, it occurs with transgression, and in Psalm 79:9, it parallels atone and is used with sin. It is striking how rarely God's salvation is connected with spiritual or moral matters. Rather, *salvation has to do with physical, material, social, and political matters.*

These findings could be further supported if we would examine yet other words which are used to talk of God's saving action. These terms too are almost always used with God's acts in the social, material, and political arena.

Thus we can sum up our study of the Hebrew material regarding God's saving actions by stressing that the words for *save* used in the Hebrew Scriptures refer to salvation from real historical, political, and material distress. These words point to the deliverance or liberation of the needy, the disadvantaged, the poor, and helpless from their oppressors.

The work of God in the Exodus is thus the pattern of God's salvation—it deals with the liberation of slaves from their foreign oppressors. This act of salvation also transforms—the oppression of the status quo is shattered. In translating this notion of God's salvation into English, *liberation* is the word which fits best. Since liberation is used primarily of people, it has political, material, and social meaning and it implies a fundamental change of the status quo. God's salvation is liberation!

Salvation and shalom justice

Now that we understand more clearly the nature of God's salvation as presented by the Hebrew Scriptures, we can better appreciate the close link between salvation and shalom justice.

In the last chapter, we saw that a major sign of shalom justice was aid flowing to those in need, regardless of merit. This is certainly the case in God's acts of salvation which we have just examined. Those who are liberated did not deserve it; in fact, they may well have deserved the oppression they were getting. This is made plain in 1 Samuel 12:9-10:

> But they forgot Yahweh their God; and [God] sold them into the hand of Sisera, commander of the army of Jabin king of Hazor, and into the hand of the Philistines, and into the hand of the king

of Moab; and they fought against them. And they cried to Yahweh, and said, "We have sinned, because we have forsaken Yahweh and have served the Baals and the Ashtaroth; but now deliver [save] us out of the hand of our enemies, and we will serve thee."

In one sense, the people were getting what they deserved as punishment for their idolatry. Nevertheless, they could pray to God for salvation from their enemies. They did not merit God's liberation; they could only request it. In response to their plea, God's act of salvation was an act of grace. It was an act based on need, not merit. This is not to deny that the oppressed may indeed have merit. It is only to say that salvation flows to those in need regardless of merit.[1]

Note in this passage, and the same would also be true elsewhere, that the people do not pray that God will save them from their sin; rather, they confess their sins and seek forgiveness for them. The salvation for which they do pray, on the other hand, is for deliverance from their oppressive social and political conditions.

This same notion is also found in God's salvation from Egypt. God's salvation was given not because Israel was so good but because God loved them, saw their oppression, and remembered the promise to their ancestors. Deuteronomy 7:7-8 says:

It was not because you were more in number than any other people that Yahweh set [God's] love upon you and chose you, for you were the fewest of all peoples; but it is because Yahweh loves you, and is keeping the oath which [was sworn to your ancestors], that Yahweh has brought you out with a mighty hand, and redeemed you from the house of bondage, from the hand of Pharaoh king of Egypt.

A bit later in Deuteronomy, we read:

Know therefore, that Yahweh your God is not giving you this good land to possess because of your righteousness; for you are a stubborn people (9:6).

The salvation from Egypt showed grace on the part of God, the liberator, who based action on their needs not their merit. From this we

---

1. One might say that the confession of sin meant they merited God's deliverance. However, confession of wrong here seems to serve as a prologue for requesting God's aid—it is not the basis for a demand of what is rightfully due them from God. Confession is a prerequisite perhaps for God's action but not a sufficient cause for it.

may conclude that *salvation / liberation is an expression of shalom justice because it is based on meeting need, not on rewarding according to merit.*

Here again we see the double-sided nature of God's shalom justice. For the oppressed, God's salvation is an expression of grace and liberation, it is vindication and freedom. For the oppressor, however, it is an act of judgment, as the Egyptians discovered all too well. So, then, *God's acts of salvation / liberation are channels for shalom justice because they transform the situation of oppression to one of freedom and liberation for the oppressed.*

Love and justice

Seeing this connection between shalom justice and God's salvation allows us to make an important connection between God's love and justice. Usually, when we think of love and justice, we see them as, in some sense, opposed to each other. Justice is what is due people, while love gives them more than they justly deserve. This contradiction between love and justice comes about when justice is understood to be based on tit for tat (reciprocity), in contrast to that which love gives regardless of merit.

Shalom justice, by contrast, is moved by love since the standard for shalom justice is not whether people deserve it but whether they need it. As we have just seen, God acting on the basis of love saves the helpless and oppressed and thereby implements shalom justice.

From this, we can understand that God's love and God's justice understood as shalom justice do not conflict. Love is the driving force, shalom justice is its end result. Since God acts to bring about this justice through salvation, salvation is at once an expression of both God's love and God's justice. When we see this link between biblical love and justice, we will not find God more concerned for one than for the other. *From a biblical point of view, God cannot be a God of love and not a God for shalom justice. God cannot be a God for justice and not be a God who acts to liberate the oppressed!*

But does not God love everyone, oppressor as well as oppressed? Of course. However, those, like the Egyptians, who refuse to repent and acknowledge God's rule by working for shalom justice block God's aim in history which is shalom. By practicing oppression, they oppose God and receive retribution for this opposition.

So too for us, our drive for shalom justice comes from love for both oppressed and oppressors. For Moses, this meant not only working with his people, the oppressed, but also confronting Pharaoh with the demand that the oppressed be set free. This seems to imply that *for us, to be a shalom maker is to act from love through justice to liberate those in bondage since only through liberation can shalom be experi-*

enced. But this love does not avoid resistance to or judgment on those who oppress and deny liberation since without liberation how can they live in shalom?

Salvation in the Greek Scriptures

So far we have been talking about God's salvation as it occurs in the Hebrew Bible. But what about the New Testament? Surely, here we will find a view of salvation more in keeping with our usual notion of what God's salvation is. Well, yes and no. As a matter of fact, the Greek word *sodzo* (to save) is used in a way similar to the way the Hebrew words for salvation are used.

Here are the statistics. *Sodzo* occurs some 111 times in the New Testament with God or Jesus almost always its subject. About half of these appear in the first three Gospels, called the Synoptic Gospels. Since these Gospels carry such a high use, and since they concern the most significant event in the New Testament, the life and teachings of Jesus, we will begin our study of salvation in the New Testament by seeing how *sodzo* is used there.

Salvation in the Synoptic Gospels

As in Hebrew, *sodzo* usually refers to deliverance from physical or material conditions. This is somewhat obscured in English translations because *sodzo* is often translated in some other way. An example of this is found in Mark 5:23, 28, 34. In verse 23, the ruler says to Jesus, "Come and lay your hands on her, so that she may be made well, and live." The word translated *made well* is *sodzo*, literally, *be saved*. So the ruler really asks, "Come and lay your hands upon her, so that she may be saved and live."

In verse 28, the woman with an issue of blood says to herself, "If I touch even his garments, I shall be made well" (literally, "I shall be saved"). Here again the reference is to deliverance from a disease: a physical, material factor. Finally, in verse 34, after the woman has been healed, Jesus says to her, "Daughter, your faith has made you well [saved you]; go in peace and be healed of your disease."

Or again, the term can be used of deliverance from the danger of physical death, as in Matthew 8:25 and 14:30; or as in Mark 15:30,31, where Jesus was taunted by some saying,

> ". . . save yourself, and come down from the cross!" So also the chief priests mocked him to one another with the scribes, saying, "He saved others; he cannot save himself."

Here they are asking Jesus to demonstrate his messiahship by saving himself from the death of crucifixion. They refer to past events in which Jesus did save others, as seen above in Mark 5.

It is striking that only in one case out of almost fifty is *sodzo* used with sin as its stated object. That usage is found in Matthew 1:21, in a comment explaining the name of Jesus—which in Hebrew means savior. Another reference where sin seems implied, though not used as the object of the verb "to save," is Luke 7:50. In the Synoptic Gospels, the meaning of salvation is quite similar to what we have seen in the Hebrew Scriptures: *salvation occurs mainly as a matter of dealing with physical, material problems. Rarely does it refer to internal, spiritual, moral defects or faults, like sin.*

Salvation in Acts and Paul

When we go to the Book of Acts[2] and the ministry of the early church, the pattern is much the same. Saving someone can refer to healing them from disease as in 4:9 or 14:9 or saving people from the peril of death as in 27:20, 31. It also occurs in general sayings, as in Acts 2:47, "And the Lord added to their number day by day those who were being saved."

In this case, along with most of the uses in Acts, no information is given as to what people are being saved from. (Other general references are Acts 4:12; 11:14; 15:1, 11; 16:30, 31.) It would seem in these cases, being saved is parallel in part to becoming a member of the Christian community but it also seems to have a theological, spiritual dimension. *For the writer of Acts, salvation is both physical and theological.*

A look at the Pauline letters will help round out our study of *sodzo* in the New Testament. Several interesting facts about *sodzo* also appear in these letters. First of all, sin almost never occurs as the stated direct object of the verb "to save"! Rather, Paul talks about being saved from the wrath of God (Rom. 5:9), or being saved in the day of the Lord Jesus (1 Cor. 5:5). (See also 3:15.) In other words, Paul views salvation as something yet to come in the future! It is future salvation (eschatological); *Paul usually uses* sodzo *in the future tense.*

But just because Paul sees salvation as future does not mean that he thought of salvation as only spiritual. This future salvation for Paul also had a material, physical sense—it was the salvation of the individual at the final judgment, as he says in 1 Corinthians 3:15:

If any [person's] work is burned up, [they] will suffer loss, though [they themselves] will be saved, but only as through fire.

---

2. While Acts forms the sequel to Luke it seemed appropriate to discuss Luke with its relatives, Matthew and Mark. Also the setting and use of *save / salvation* is somewhat different in Acts than in Luke as will be apparent. This, I hope, justifies separating them in my discussion of salvation.

Here being saved is the opposite of perishing, of being burned up. The word is used in this sense again in the present tense in 1 Corinthians 1:18 where the contrast is between those who are being saved, as over against those who are perishing.

Returning now to the general references in Acts, some of which are also in the future tense, it would seem that they are likewise being used eschatologically, referring to salvation / deliverance at the end of time from the punishment / wrath of God. If this is the case, these uses may also refer to physical, material, bodily salvation since it is the whole person who is being delivered from suffering God's wrath.

We can conclude, then, that for Paul and the early church as portrayed in Acts, a physical, material component to being saved was implied. Sometimes this salvation was pushed to the end of time. Here is where the Christian would finally be fully vindicated by God's justice and would fully experience salvation, the final liberation from all need. But, and this is the point to be stressed, while in the New Testament salvation becomes much more future oriented, it is still a physical, material salvation. See the last chapter of Revelation, for example, with its city, water, trees, people, and nations. This is a picture of physical, social, and political life transformed by the saving power of God. Thus I believe it is a false equation to see future salvation as only a spiritual salvation.[3]

Salvation elsewhere in the New Testament

What we found in the Synoptic Gospels, in Acts, and in the Letters of Paul is also typical of the rest of the New Testament; *sodzo* (save) is used for liberation from physical, material problems or threats. For example, in the Book of James we find salvation as liberation from physical disease. In 5:15, it says, "and the prayer of faith will save the sick man." This is closely related to uses we have seen in the Synoptic Gospels. Side by side with this, we find in 5:20 a usage pointing to the future:

> Let him know that whoever brings back a sinner from the error
> of his way will save his soul [*psyche*] from death and will cover a
> multitude of sins.

This passage seems to refer to our more usual notion of spiritual salvation, the salvation of the soul from sin. But this is not necessarily the case, since in the New Testament the word translated soul (*psyche*) means life or the whole person as in Acts 27:20, 31 where it refers to people, whole physical persons, being saved from shipwreck. Also,

3. See Carlos H. Abesamis, *Where Are We Going: Heaven or New World?* (Manila: Communications Foundation for Asia, 1983).

from a biblical point of view, the body will be resurrected, so a whole person, body and all, will either be saved or perish in the day of the Lord. Thus we should probably translate here as: "will save their life from death."

Now the point being made in this section is not that salvation does not have any spiritual or interior component; salvation does include this aspect of the person in some references. Rather, it is to be stressed that the Bible frequently, even usually, talks about salvation as material, physical liberation or deliverance. This biblical emphasis should not be neglected; we should not limit salvation to just one aspect of the person, the spiritual as opposed to the physical; the whole person, body, mind, and spirit is to be liberated. *Biblical salvation is thus total, it includes liberation of the whole person; not just the physical, although this is the part of the person usually directly affected by biblical salvation, nor the spiritual to the neglect of physical liberation.*[4]

Thus when we limit salvation to only a spiritual concept, when we think of salvation only as the saving of some soul which has a separate existence of its own apart from the person's total being, we no longer have a full-bodied biblical salvation, but a disembodied view of salvation. This is not how the Hebrew Scriptures talk about God's salvation, nor is it how the Synoptic Gospels talk about Jesus' saving works. *Biblical salvation is liberation for the whole person, both materially and spiritually.*

It is significant, in this regard, that when Moses first confronted Pharaoh, he asked for a three-day journey out of Egypt so that the oppressed Israelites could worship. Evidently, being in bondage was a detriment to the worship of God, because if worship was only a spiritual matter, why did Israel need to leave its state of oppression to worship God?

The totality of salvation is important because limiting salvation to a spiritual and soul salvation does not necessarily lead to shalom. If only saving a nonphysical entity, the soul, is what is called for, then salvation can go with all sorts of material injustice and oppression—one can be busy saving souls without paying any attention to liberation from physical oppression and exploitation which we have seen is an object of God's salvation. Indeed, this is all too often what happens, especially when this type of salvation is preached by the more affluent and, yes, the oppressors, to the less affluent and oppressed. One can find this

---

4. For a study of salvation in the Bible which demonstrates the biblical emphasis on future salvation as total salvation see Abesamis, *Where Are We Going: Heaven or New World?* He has a helpful chapter comparing traditional ideas of salvation and the ones we find in the Bible. His work is an important supplement to the present chapter since he draws heavily on Jesus' teachings on the kingdom of God, which I have omitted here. His work should be read in connection with this chapter.

version of the gospel in every third-world country. This is not the gospel of shalom.

In the Bible, however, we have seen that God's salvation is not one which expresses concern only for people's suffering in the next world but does nothing about people's oppression and suffering in this world, their present hell. God's salvation is meant to be a present reality, aimed at liberation here and now. It is to liberate those presently being oppressed, to heal those presently ill! God's judgment, we have seen, stands against all who would hold back this liberation.

The biblical message of salvation means transformation of the present, an end to the oppressions of the status quo. Without this transformation, from a biblical point of view, salvation is incomplete and shalom is lacking.

What happened to sin?

Just because the Bible does not usually use *save* or *salvation* with sin, but rather with physical ills and political oppression, does not mean that it does not take sin seriously. It does. But the Bible uses another set of words to talk about sin.

The most frequent word used with sin, in both Testaments, is *forgive*. Sin is something that is forgiven. Sin hinders a relationship between people or between people and God. The guilty party, the one who has injured the relationship asks for forgiveness and the offended party grants forgiveness, thereby restoring the relationship to wholeness. In Hebrew Scriptures, for example, idolatry was a sin—it broke the relationship with God—and needed God's forgiveness in order to restore the relationship.

Besides the words of forgiveness, words from the rites of sacrifice are also used: *expiate* or *atone, bear sin,* or *carry off.* In the Hebrew Scriptures, of course, these words refer to the effect of animal sacrifices. In the New Testament, these words apply to the death of Christ.

Finally, a set of words borrowed from the legal sphere of life are used with sin. Here belong words like *ransom,* which means to secure the release of someone through payment, or *redeem,* which has a similar meaning, as in "redeeming a pledge." Thus sin was a serious matter, it marred relationships, held people in bondage, and kept shalom from being realized. Sin had to be erased and blotted out.

We will not discuss the nature of sin here. We will postpone this topic to the next chapter on the atonement. What we simply want to point out, in order to avoid any misunderstanding, is that sin is a serious problem and is dealt with in the Bible in a variety of ways but the vocabulary for salvation is not one of these major ways.

However, it is important to note here for our understanding of salvation that a person's view of sin seems related to that person's idea of salvation. When one sees salvation as a spiritual, individual, and interior matter, this relates to a certain view of sin—it is also individual. But if it is a sin to oppress others and oppression is a sign of sin, liberating the oppressed from their oppressors deals a blow to sin and is understood as salvation.

Furthermore, since sin, as more generally understood, especially in Paul, is bondage, salvation puts an ax to the roots of sin by liberating from all bondages and by transforming all sinful structures which enslave. As Paul puts it in Romans 6:17, once you were slaves of sin. But from this bondage, we are called to freedom—to be free people (Gal. 5:1).

However, the notion of personal, interior sin is an important one which we dare not brush aside or discount. It is understood that some bondage is more open than others—appearing in social structures and relationships. Other forms of bondage are rooted in the mind and heart—sexism, racism, and feudalism, for example. These binding and oppressing habits of thought are tied, of course, to certain social and economic structures with which they grow and expand, and, indeed, they reinforce each other. As a result, both forms of bondage need to be taken into account and both need to be dealt with. It seems to me that neither approach is good enough by itself—to try to change the mind and heart without changing the structures in society or to try to change the structures without including the need for personal change. Biblical salvation as freedom from bondage can cover both: deliverance from the physical, material conditions of oppression and from the habits of thought which feed on and foster this oppression.

Thus in English usage where we usually connect salvation with deliverance from sin, we should remember that salvation is for all, although it may take different forms, depending on the the forms of sin and bondage. The inner transforming of the mind parallels the outer reshaping of social structures which are oppressive. These are not separate salvations because sin, disobedience to God's intentions for shalom and justice, is at the root of both. Salvation from sin becomes then a process and struggle for both personal and social change—the two should not be separated in practice.

To return again to the example of Moses and the Israelites, it was not enough to physically liberate them from Egypt, but they also needed to be freed from their slave mentality which expressed itself in their repeated longing to return to Egypt and to slavery again. *In this perspective, understanding sin biblically as bondage and oppression, we may continue to talk about salvation as salvation from sin remembering that sin is manifested in human bondage; salvation liberates people from their plight both through transformation of minds and hearts and through transformation of social structures. Neither by itself is adequate.*

After all this, the question arises: why has our understanding of salvation become so different from what we see talked about in the Bible as salvation? One oversimplified guess at what has happened to the notion of salvation in the church is that sin became the focal issue, especially personal sin, guilt, and how an individual can enter a right relationship with God.[5] The forgiveness of sin and the restoring of relationship with God so that one would go to heaven became the focus of the church and was referred to as being saved. Thus salvation became an individual, interior, spiritual, and future matter. What had earlier been treated by salvation—liberation from physical ills and social oppression thus fell outside the church's notion of salvation. As a result, it was not seen as central to the church nor something to which the church should devote major energy and attention.

This tendency was aided to some extent by doctrines of the atonement. We will turn to the atonement in the next chapter in order to understand it in the broader context of shalom justice and salvation. More will be said there about sin, structures, and personal transformation. What seems clear so far is that God's salvation is clearly shown in both the Old and New Testaments as liberation, as dealing with social, political, and physical problems. This *aspect* of salvation we dare not ignore if we are to have a biblical view of salvation.

5. The classic statement on how Western Christianity since the Reformation has read Paul personalistically is Krister Stendahl's article, "The Apostle Paul and the Introspective Conscience of the West," *Harvard Theological Review* 56(1963)199ff.

5. *The atonement: an act of God's justice*

B y examining the Exodus and the words used for salvation in the Bible, we found a view quite different from our usual understanding of salvation. We often regard salvation as a spiritual, internal, and otherworldly transaction which has to do with God and the person's relation with God. It has little to do with the actual physical life and circumstances of the individual.

This contrasts sharply with what we found stressed in the Bible: salvation as material and political deliverance—salvation as liberation. Where did our spiritual, personalistic view of salvation come from? What is its biblical basis? How does it relate to salvation as liberation? To probe these questions, we need to explore the more traditional understandings of salvation. While we cannot touch on every detail, we aim to cover the main points, suggest further lines of thought, and point to the importance of shalom for understanding salvation.

Theories of the atonement

The Bible describes two central acts of salvation: the first is the Exodus and the second is the life, death, and resurrection of Jesus. Our traditional Christian views of salvation are largely based upon an interpretation of what happened in or through this second act: the life, death, and resurrection of Jesus. Since the New Testament itself has no single well-defined interpretation of what happened as a result of Jesus' death, the church, over the years, has developed several theories. We will first look briefly at these various ideas of the atonement in order to lay a foundation for our traditional understanding of salvation.

We also want to go a step beyond these usual views by placing the atonement in its wider biblical context. We do this in order to understand how the salvation which we see God bringing in Jesus is similar to what God is doing elsewhere, as in the Exodus. Should we not expect that the work of God's salvation is a continuing work with a common purpose throughout history? The means may change, but would not God's purpose and goal remain the same? Thus, in looking at the work of Jesus as an act of salvation, we will try to discover how the Bible's understanding of this event is connected to its understanding of God's justice and saving actions elsewhere.

Making the atonement one of the general biblical themes along with salvation, justice, and shalom is an important point. In the past, the atonement has often been treated apart from these major ingredients of biblical faith. This has happened, perhaps, for two reasons. First, because, in explaining what happened in Jesus' death, Roman ideas of justice were used, sometimes placing the atonement in a nonbiblical framework, which gave a different twist to it. Second, since the atonement is so central to Christian faith, such an understanding of the atonement, once accepted, then came to dominate our interpretation and understanding of the rest of the Bible. It would seem to be a case of the tail wagging the dog!

Our procedure here has been just the opposite. We first brought out the wider biblical view of justice and salvation before tackling the atonement. So, we will now try to understand atonement within this wider biblical context.

From the standpoint of the church today, we might consider the atonement at the heart of what God is about. Yet the church had no official or well-formed doctrine of the atonement for its first 1,000 years. It was only later that various views of the atonement were written to be accepted or rejected by the church.

One of the reasons for this delayed development of a doctrine of the atonement may be in the variety of metaphors or word pictures used in the New Testament for the work of Christ. Jesus referred to his life being given as a *ransom* in Mark 10:45; Paul uses *expiation* in Romans 3:24-26; *reconciliation* in 2 Corinthians 5:18; *redemption by becoming a curse* in Galatians 3:13; in Ephesians 1:5-10, a variety of terms and images are used: *becoming God's children, redemption, forgiveness of sins*, and *uniting all* through Jesus' death. More word pictures could be added to this list. One thing seems clear: the New Testament had no single way in which it described the effects of the death of Christ.

These words or metaphors are taken from various spheres of life. They may be looked upon as a series of windows which biblical writers used to give us a view of what was effected in Jesus death; however, no single one of these word windows allows us to see the whole. Each window plays its part in letting us see part of the whole, but none shows it all. Problems arise when the view from one word window is taken to be the whole view or the only one. It becomes the full view rather than a window to a reality beyond. When this is done, the biblical witness is skewed because the focus becomes too narrow.

So, it would seem better to build a theory of the atonement on those passages in which the New Testament describes the results of Jesus' death, rather than to use only or mainly word windows, like *ransom* or *expiation*. Using several descriptive passages, such as Romans 5:1-11, and the wider background of the themes of justice, salvation, and shalom, we will present a supplemental perspective on the atonement which is offered as an enrichment to the traditional theories.[1] But first, a survey, for the sake of perspective, of the three major traditional views.

The satisfaction or substitutionary theory

The satisfaction or substitutionary view was developed in 1097 in a book by Anselm entitled *Cur Deos Homo?* (Why the God Man?). This book tried to answer the question of why the incarnation was necessary: why did God need to become human? The answer came by way of a theory of the atonement—God became human so that a human could die and thereby gain salvation for us.

Now why was it necessary for the God-man to die to do this? Anselm explained it thus: People are sinners, they have rebelled against God, and thereby have offended God. People, because of their sin, are guilty and deserve to be punished by God. Thus, all people stand under God's wrath and judgment. This is the problem: how do we deal with God's wrath which rests upon us? People themselves are not able to give God satisfaction, make restitution, so to speak, for their wrong. Nothing they can do will remove the wrath of God from them. Neither can God forgive them, because this would go against the moral order: it would be unjust. This is the dilemma in which people and God find themselves: people are unable to repay God and God is prevented by justice from forgiving them their debt.

Jesus, however, was able to solve the problem. As divine, he was able to live a life without sin. He owed God no debt. As debt free, he could offer himself as a substitute for us, accept our punishment. God's wrath, which we deserved, was vented on Jesus. God's justice is now satisfied, the debt has been paid. We individually received release from our punishment by a transfer of the merits of Jesus' death to us. By this transfer, we became right with God and thus escaped the doom which our own deeds would have brought upon us.

1. There is a great deal of literature on the atonement. I have found the following especially helpful in presenting different points of view: Gustaf Aulen, *Christus Victor: An Historical Study of the Three Main Types of the Idea of Atonement*, trans. A. G. Herbert (New York: Macmillan Co., 1951); H. G. Link, "Reconciliation, Restoration, Propitiation, Atonement," in *New International Dictionary of New Testament Theology* III, 145-76; Gordon Kaufman, *Systematic Theology: A Historicist Perspective* (New York: Charles Scribner's Sons, 1968), pp. 389-410; Martin Hengel, *The Atonement: The Origins of the Doctrine in the New Testament*, trans. John Bowden (Philadelphia: Fortress Press, 1981); John Howard Yoder *Preface to Theology: Christology and Theological Method* (Elkhart, Ind.: Co-op Bookstore of Goshen Biblical Seminary, n. d.); John Driver, *Understanding the Atonement from a Believer's Church Perspective*, unpublished manuscript.

This transfer of merits from Jesus to us, Jesus' atonement for our sins, happens either through the sacraments or by faith, depending upon our religious tradition. For Catholics, the sacraments make salvation effective for the individual; in much of Protestantism, it is the faith of the individual which makes this transfer happen.

This is probably the prevailing view of the atonement today; for most Christians, it represents orthodoxy. While this view has strengths and it does build on ways the New Testament talks about Jesus' death, it does not represent New Testament teaching in all respects. Basically this understanding of the atonement places Jesus' death within the context of punishing justice (also known as retributive justice), rather than within the context of shalom justice. According to the satisfaction view, we deserve to be punished because we have done wrong. God is unable to forgive us, because this would be a failure of retributive justice. But the New Testament sees the atonement as based on shalom justice, not retributive justice. Paul in Romans 5:6-11 says:

> While we were still weak, at the right time Christ died for the ungodly. Why, one will hardly die for a righteous man—though perhaps for a good man one will dare even to die. But God shows his love for us in that while we were yet sinners Christ died for us. Since, therefore, we are now justified by his blood, much more shall we be saved by him from the wrath of God. For if while we were enemies we were reconciled to God by the death of his Son, much more, now that we are reconciled, shall we be saved by his life. Not only so, but we also rejoice in God through our Lord Jesus Christ, through whom we have now received our reconciliation.

Paul describes the state of people as weak, ungodly, sinners, and enemies. Being sinners, we were in need of help, but we could not help ourselves because we were weak. Furthermore, we did not deserve help being enemies of God. Thus God acted out of love, in order to meet our need. Here we have a description of shalom justice—meeting people's needs, based not on their merits, but on God's love. As seen in the chapter on justice, shalom justice does not cancel punishment, especially for those who oppress and block shalom justice. So here we have the wrath of God, God's punishing justice. But this aspect of justice must be seen within the context of God's purpose in Jesus for shalom justice: God's desire for all to be reconciled and have shalom. It is not God's will that any should perish: God extends reconciliation and shalom justice to all. The fact that all will not accept the offer, does not diminish the offer, nor its nature.

When, however, the atonement is viewed as retributive justice rather than as shalom justice, Jesus becomes the agent who brings about justice, he is the one who reconciles us to God. God becomes the object, the stern judge operating according to punishing justice, who needs to be pacified. This conception represents the opposite of what is stated in 2 Corinthians 5:18-21, namely, that God was in Christ reconciling the world to God's self. There Jesus is the instrument of an involved God. God is the subject who is doing the reconciling. This is the consistent witness of the New Testament: God is the agent of reconciliation, not its object.

Further, in the substitutionary view of the atonement, we find a separation between atonement and ethics, between being reconciled to God and living the life of reconciliation. It seems clear, in Paul, at least, that the atonement meant a transfer of lordships, from the realm of sin and death into Jesus the Christ. Indeed, *in Christ* is the term Paul uses most often to say what it means to be a Christian. (See Rom. 8:2, 39; 12:5; 1 Cor. 15:22; 2 Cor. 5:17; Gal. 2:4; 3:14, 28, for a sample.) Thus it was not only a matter of retributive justice, dealing with a debt which we incurred, but a change of life commitment, a change of orientation.

This Paul states most clearly in Romans 6:17-22. Here he says that Jesus came so that we might live under a new master, liberated from bondage to the old. What is important in the atonement is that a person is now in Christ, a member of the body of Christ. The lack of attention to this New Testament emphasis has at times led to the notion that the atonement is a legal fiction: God treats us as just, but we are still the same old sinners. On this, the New Testament is clear—we are not the same old sinners. If we remain in sin, then we are not in Christ, and if we are not in Christ, then Jesus died in vain.

Lastly, this view represents what has been called a cradle-grave christology. What is important, it seems to imply, is that Jesus was born so that he could die. Who he was in history as the messiah of God, what he taught, and how he lived are all, in a sense, irrelevant to salvation. But the example of Jesus' life is important in the New Testament. Indeed, even Jesus' suffering is seen as a model or example and not just as a theological event.

In 1 Thessalonians 1:6, Paul says that when the Thessalonians became Christians they also became imitators of him and of Jesus, and in that they too "received the word in much affliction." Or Paul writes about himself in Galatians 6:17, "Henceforth let no man trouble me; for I bear on my body the marks of Jesus." Again in Philippians 3:10, "that I may know him and the power of his resurrection, and may share his sufferings, becoming like him in his death." Paul makes a clear connection between his own experience and the suffering of Jesus.

Along this line, Paul writes in 2 Corinthians 1:5-6:

> For as we share abundantly in Christ's sufferings, so through Christ we share abundantly in comfort too. If we are afflicted, it is for your comfort and salvation; and if we are comforted, it is for your comfort, which you experience when you patiently endure the same sufferings that we suffer.

It seems clear that the sufferings of Christ had not only theological meaning but had practical significance as an example. His followers could also expect to suffer, and to suffer for one another, just as Jesus suffered for them. This aspect of Jesus' death and resurrection can be undervalued by a cradle-grave christology because by giving events theological meaning, it can detract from their historical and ethical significance, narrowing the focus of Jesus' work and thereby failing to grasp its full impact.

But by placing the atonement in the context of shalom justice, as we did above, a contradiction seems to emerge. Earlier, we used shalom justice most often to talk about physical need, ending oppression, freeing slaves, and healing the sick. The atonement does not seem to be directed to these needs but rather toward a theological, nonphysical dimension: toward liberation from the bondage of sin and toward reconciliation with God. How does this relate to shalom justice? How does this put rice on the table of the poor and hungry? How does it free those oppressed by poverty?

As pointed out in the last chapter, liberation from sin involves both a change in attitudes and values, and structural changes which reflect and reinforce the new values. Insofar as the atonement empowers conversion—a change of mind and perspective—the atonement also empowers structural, social transformation. That a change of mind *is* necessary is eloquently witnessed to by the need to convince the oppressed that they must act in order that social change may be brought about. Without a conversion of mind—without conscientization—is any real transformation likely in the long run?

It seems to me, then, that the atonement not only illustrates God's work of shalom justice—meeting human need without regard to merit—but is part of what we have seen elsewhere. The atonement focuses more on the individual, which this view of the atonement stresses, and freedom from old personal bondages of mind and heart, while the Exodus, for example, focuses more on the group and social change. Granted the necessity of both transformations for real change, conversion is necessary if the poor are to have rice on the table. It is to the need for this personal conversion that this, and other views of the atonement, point.

The moral influence theory

Another theory of the atonement, which gained a following, came from Abelard, who lived a short while after Anselm. It can be understood in part as a reaction to the coldness, distance, and wrathfulness of God in Anselm's view. It also places increased stress on what happens to the individual.

In this view, God is a God of love who does not need to be appeased. Certainly, this is an important aspect of New Testament teaching—God is at work through Jesus because of love not because of wrath. Perhaps the clearest statement of this in the New Testament is 1 John 4:10:

> In this is love, not that we loved God but that he loved us and sent his Son to be the expiation for our sins. (See also John 3:16.)

But people have rejected God and live in disobedience in spite of God's love. They find themselves in sin and alienated from God. But if by faith, people experience God's love through Jesus' death, love is awakened in their hearts and transforms them. A bond of love now comes to unite them with God and with their fellows. This love which is awakened in their hearts is the basis of their justification. Second Corinthians 5:14-17 expresses this idea in stating that people's lives are controlled by Christ's love, once they realize why Jesus died on the cross: so that all might live under Christ's lordship.

This view of the atonement is also known as the subjective view, since what happens, happens within people; it is a subjective change in the way they feel and view the world. The substitutionary view on the other hand is known as the objective view: Jesus' death provides the objective removal of our debt to God. This is not something which happens inside of us, but is a change in outside reality; our debt is removed and we are no longer debtors.

While the accent on God's love and human transformation is an essential biblical theme and corrects some of the tendencies of the substitutionary view, this theory also has its weaknesses. It does not account well for why Jesus had to die. Why did an innocent man have to die to show us love? Could God not have found another way to show love toward us? Here the substitutionary view seems stronger.

God's role in the process also tends to become secondary, since we are transformed by the example and death of Jesus. God seems to be a bystander who watches the drama, but is not intimately involved. This is a weakness which we also saw in the previous view. However, as shown above, it seems clear from the New Testament that God was actively involved, God was the agent, who "was in Christ reconciling the world to himself, not counting their trespasses against them" (2 Cor. 5:19).

Finally, this view does not seem to take sin and evil seriously enough. God's wrath will be directed toward those who persist in sin. It seems to slight the deeper problem of sin as a problem of the human will and sinful structures within which people live. Even though we know and want to do what is right and loving, we often end up doing evil since we are part of evil situations or structures. The sin of oppression, for example, is not so much overcome by people being nice, loving people, but by transforming the structures of oppression into ones which allow love to be expressed through shalom justice.

The classical theory

These two theories or explanations of the atonement have dominated the church for the last 700 years or so. But neither theory seemed completely adequate as shown above. As a result, in this century, another theory has been proposed. Although its present form is the work of the Swedish scholar Gustaf Aulen, he contends that in fact this view represents the implied understanding of the early church and the early church fathers. Although they never developed such a theory, he finds it embedded in their writings. This is why he calls it the classic view—it was the original view of the church until the time of Anselm and Abelard, whose views tended to displace it.

According to this view, a battle is raging, a battle between good and evil. People find themselves held in the power of evil, in bondage to Satan. The evil which holds them expresses itself both personally in the evil acts which people do, as well as corporately in the evil expressed in the institutions of society and the patterns of social interaction, like racism, sexism, and classism.

As a result, we find ourselves enslaved by powers from which we cannot free ourselves. As an individual, I find myself doing evil. As I take part in my society and its institutions, I am a partner in even greater evil. A real strength of this theory is that it takes the New Testament view of sin and evil seriously. Sin, especially in the Pauline writings, is a power or force which enslaves. It is not just a matter of doing misdeeds. Furthermore, sin exists in forces which control societies: the principalities and powers, the forces of this world. The problem of sin is not solved just by forgiving individual debts. People need to be liberated from sin's power over their lives. This also means dealing with the social dimensions of sin.

This wider view of sin and God's actions to deal with it are based on New Testament passages like Galatians 1:4 which talks about being delivered from the present evil age, or the battle imagery which we find in 1 Corinthians 15:22-26 where it is said that eventually Christ will subject all the powers to God. This classic view takes seriously the New Testament language about the ongoing battle between Jesus and the forces of evil, with the ultimate victory belonging to God when all powers submit to God's rule.

This emphasis on the New Testament teaching for the need of release from sin understood as powerful forces which control our lives and institutions is an important one. Traditionally, atonement theories have not taken the scope and extent of sin seriously enough. Sin is much more than personal misdeeds for which we feel sorrow. Sin has to do with the values and orientation by which we live—the powers which control our lives like materialism, feudalism, and greed. Before we can be liberated and before we can build the social structures of liberation we need to be freed from the control of these forces and the structures which embody them and keep them alive. This view of the atonement reinforces our discussion above about the need for both inner change and the change of structures which express and promote sin and oppression. *Jesus died to liberate.*

Jesus, in this view, however, has already, in principle, triumphed over the evil powers in his resurrection. God placed Jesus into the hands of the devil. In return, the devil released the rest of humanity which he held captive. In a sense, a bargain was struck between God and the devil; God paid the devil with Jesus and got the release of humanity in return. This notion of Jesus as a ransom takes its cue from passages like Mark 10:45 where Jesus says that he came to give his life as a ransom for many. But the devil was fooled. Jesus does not remain in his clutches, but rises victoriously from the grave. Thus, the devil is cheated of his prize.

This means that the resurrection of Jesus is the visible sign that the powers can be overcome, and, at the end of the age, they will at last be defeated. We live our lives then in a time when this victory is in the process of being worked out. The end is not here, so all the powers of oppression have not yet been removed; but the outcome is certain: one day they will be. In the midst of our struggle to ever expand the power and scope of God's liberating work, we live in hope and faith—one day the final victory will come.

One of the strengths, then, of this view is that it places the death of Christ in the stream of our own work and struggle. The victory has been won over the powers: that is the witness of the resurrection. But we have not yet gained the results of that victory—that will come in the future. In the meantime, we find ourselves caught up in the battle between the forces of bondage and oppression and the force of God's liberating love and justice. As Christians, we are on God's side in this struggle against the forces which hold people in slavery.

It would seem, then, that this third view is a powerful one, one which fits with much of what we have seen elsewhere. However, there are also weaknesses in this theory. It is perhaps too dualistic—evil is given too much power: God must respect the claims of the devil over humanity. If God is indeed sovereign, did Jesus really need to die in order to pay off the devil? Hasn't God set the limits and powers of evil? Thus, like the moral influence theory, it does not seem to give a good reason for Jesus' death.

Secondly, it strikes many as morally offensive that our redemption from sin is gotten through a fraud which God put over on the devil. Did God really need to stoop to dishonesty in order to set us free from our bondage to sin?

Thus, although this view helps balance the other two by taking into account a most important New Testament theme: the battle between God and the social and cultural forces of evil—the principalities and powers—nevertheless, it too has its shortcomings.

Summary of the traditional views of the atonement

By pointing out several things which these traditional views of the atonement have in common, we will set the stage for our further discussion of the atonement within the context of biblical faith.

First, the death of Jesus tends to be unrelated to his teachings and life. We have, as mentioned above, a cradle-cross christology. This can distort the meaning of Jesus' death if it removes it from its place and meaning in history. The death of Jesus needs to be understood as a historic event, a real part of his life. This is not meant to be an either / or argument—either Jesus' teachings and life or his death and resurrection. Rather it is simply to say that these events took place as part of a longer life and it is helpful to understand them in that light. In some sense, all three of the views do link life and death. For example, it is important for the first view that Jesus lived a perfect life as the requirement for his being able to die in our stead.

Second, the atonement is not fully a part of the larger scope of God's purposes and actions as described elsewhere in the Bible. The tendency is to make the atonement unique and place it in a theological vacuum; because it is unique in its meaning, it is not to be compared to other events. We need to balance this tendency with the view that God's action in Jesus, though unique, probably does not differ from or contradict God's other actions for justice and salvation.

Third, sin and the work of Jesus tend to be seen as touching only the life of an individual. As a result, the social effects of the atonement can be neglected or regarded as only side issues. The nature of sin that goes beyond the personal is, however, stressed by the ransom theory which can link the atonement with God's acts of liberating salvation elsewhere. This view is important both for understanding the New Testament notion of sin and the atonement as freedom from bondage.

Finally, a concern of the traditional views is to explain why an innocent victim had to die. But if we ask, could not God have shown love in some other way? is this the only way the devil could be appeased? is a God who requires a perfectly innocent party to die so that God in turn can forgive the guilty parties a just God? we do not seem to find answers that wholly satisfy. The traditional views only fulfill their own expectations in part. By placing Jesus' death in its context, we will look for more historical answers which also make connections with the larger biblical view.

The messianic view of the atonement[2]

Here we will try to supplement, not replace, the views just discussed. Also, it should be noted that just as the above views left certain ends untied, so too the following presentation does not pretend to be complete or the only possible view. Rather, it points a way, which tends to be neglected, toward understanding the work and teaching of Jesus within the scope of the broader biblical message and what we can see there of God's purposes in history.

What we are calling the messianic understanding of the atonement begins from the basic confession about Jesus—he was God's messiah who came to set up God's righteous rule on earth, God's kingdom of justice and peace. Indeed, that Jesus was the Christ (the Greek word for messiah) was the earliest and most widespread confession about Jesus. In fact, the phrase *Jesus Christ* occurs so often in the New Testament, we might almost regard it as a proper name, a first name and a last name. However, this phrase is a confession: Jesus is the Christ, the Messiah. This was the bedrock of the early church's understanding of Jesus and indeed it probably goes back to Jesus himself. For as Hengel[3] points out:

> The appearance of the risen Jesus is therefore in no way an adequate foundation for his messiahship and for the later development of christology, nor does it give a satisfactory explanation of them. . . . If Jesus had no messianic features at all, the origin of the Christian kerygma [preaching] would remain completely inexplicable and mysterious.

2. This presentation rests on the pioneering work of John Howard Yoder in *The Politics of Jesus*. Duane Friesen, professor at Bethel College, has drawn from this book the insights it offers about the atonement. I have taken these, and elaborated them somewhat. Thus the views presented below are heavily dependent on the work of Yoder and Friesen, but should not be taken as precise statements of their views.

3. Martin Hengel, *The Atonement: the Origins of the Doctrine in the New Testament*, pp. 41, 48.

As a result, what Jesus, as the messiah, taught and did was not just a filler to take up the time from his birth to his death: it was an integral part of what he was about on this earth—the proclamation of the kingdom of God. Indeed, his life illuminates his death, just as his death and resurrection confirm the claims of his life. He died as the messiah and his resurrection, in part, proved this claim.

How did this shocking thing come to be, that the messiah ended up crucified? We can understand this result when we understand Jesus' message as the messianic message of the kingdom of God. It was a message of justice; good news for the poor and oppressed, good news for human restoration. We shall have more to say about the content of Jesus' teaching below in the chapter on Jesus the Messiah. For our purposes here, it is enough to note that Jesus' message as reported by the Gospel writers is marked by an urgency, the kingdom of God is here or near in the message and person of Jesus. (See Mark 1:14-15; Luke 4:17-21; 10:5-9; 17:20-21).[4] As a result, now is the time of decision, the time of repentance and transformation. The rich should give their money to the poor and people should seek to serve rather than to dominate.

But in living out this good news as well as proclaiming it, Jesus clashed with the dominant values of the elite. (See Luke 16:14-15 for his economic teaching as alienating, 19:45-48 for his economic and political action.) As a result, the religious, political, and economic establishment came to oppose him and to plot his death. Jesus was a threat to the established order and their positions of power.

In this clash, Jesus struggles from the beginning to the end of his ministry with the question of means. At the beginning, Satan tempts him with political power, wonder working, and sustenance providing. Jesus renounces these but the temptation returns at the end. He prays in the garden that he will not have to suffer death as a result of the clash between himself and the authorities. But when his disciples act to rescue him at his arrest, he resists their use of violence on his behalf. Instead, he claims that if he wanted to use force, he has more than twelve legions of angels available to fight for him (Matt. 26:47-56).

Jesus submits, suffers, and dies on a cross rather than try to impose the messianic order by military or political means. That the messiah who was to be a victorious king would die at Roman hands, let alone die on the cross, was unheard of and on the face of it discredited Jesus' messianic claims. As Paul writes later, the cross is a stumbling block for the Jews and foolishness for the rest of us, for through it Jesus demonstrated that he was accursed of God (1 Cor. 1:23; Gal. 3:13). Thus, Jesus'

---

4. I have profited from E. P. Sanders' treatment of the message of Jesus, especially on the kingdom, in his book, *Jesus and Judaism*.

death, as portrayed in the Gospels, resulted from historical, political reactions to his life and ministry and from his own refusal to use political and military means to sustain and prolong that ministry. (See John 6:15.)

God, however, raised him from the dead as a sign that Jesus' way of suffering love resulted in victory over the powers of evil and oppression. Even death, the ultimate power over human life, was defeated. (See 1 Cor. 15:12-57.) The resurrection represents God's vindication of Jesus' messianic teaching, life, and death as a way to victory over the powers and principalities of sin and oppression. Here, as Paul writes, are the firstfruits, the harbinger of the victory and liberation which one day will come. We live and struggle in expectation of this victory even though we do not experience it in its full expression now. We have noted the stress which the classic view places on this aspect of the atonement: Jesus' work is meant to empower liberation from the forces and structure of evil as we meet them in our world today.

Furthermore, since, in his death, Jesus absorbed evil, God's power is shown in the absorption of evil. The cross thereby became the ultimate symbol of God's saving power expressed through love for enemies as Romans 5:1-11 points out.

From this passage in Romans, we also see that the cross, motivated by love, is an act of God to set things right. The cross, thereby, illustrates the basic nature and pattern of God's salvation as we have seen elsewhere in the Bible—it aims to set things right. Here this pattern is applied to a different level, the theological domain, making things all right between people and God.

From this point of view, we should understand justification not as punishing justice but as shalom justice—justification is liberation from sin in order that things may be right.[5] It is important to note in Romans 5:1-11 that reconciliation and the establishment of peace result from justification. That is, since shalom justice makes things okay, there is now a basis for reconciliation and peace. Too often our idea of reconciliation is that it sets things right between people when, in fact, things are not okay. The death of Jesus points to the need for setting things right—in this case, with God—in order that we might have peace and reconciliation. Less than that is a whitewash of the status quo. *Jesus did not die to leave the status quo untouched; his death made a difference.*

This theological language may appear to contradict our earlier study which found that *save* and *salvation* are not primarily used to talk about sin and a relationship with God but about physical, material

---

5. I have found E. P. Sanders' discussion of justification, and of Paul's thinking more generally, extremely illuminating and helpful. See his *Paul and Palestinian Judaism: A Comparison of Patterns of Religion* (Philadelphia: Fortress Press, 1977).

matters. At first glance, then, a certain gap does appear. What does connect with our previous study of salvation, however, is that the atonement is an expression of shalom justice because it models meeting need. The need in this case is the need for freedom from the power of sin (as discussed above), so that people may be reconciled to God, gain a new orientation (being in Christ, putting on the new), and create the new social conditions which reflect this reconciliation and orientation. As discussed above, the atonement, by dealing with the more personal parts of conversion which are necessary for real change and liberation, fulfills and empowers God's purposes seen elsewhere in God's acts of salvation in history. Understood in this way, the atonement connects with God's other acts of salvation and shalom justice. We will comment further on this below.

What does it mean that Jesus' death was an act of shalom justice which liberates? For Paul, this act transfers us from the realm of sin and death to the realm of Christ and life. Sin (in Paul's writings, it is usually sin rather than sins) is a power that controls human life. (See Rom. 6.) It is a force which enslaves people and expresses itself in a variety of ways. Some of these, as we have suggested, are racism, sexism, materialism, feudalism, and classism. For people to be free and create a free society, they need to be liberated from these forces which bind them: liberated internally from these habits of thought and externally from structures which reinforce and express them through oppression and alienation. The cross of Jesus provides the power for people to become free from them by having new minds and wills to live a new kind of life. This life is expressed in a new set of relationships and socioeconomic structures which replace the old values and relationships that belong to oppression, greed, and the will to dominate. As a result, our lives are transformed because we are set free from our bondage to sin's power (2 Cor. 5:14-17; Rom. 6) and we struggle toward structures which reflect our new consciousness.

How does Jesus' death on the cross accomplish this? Jesus' death enables our doing shalom justice because God's love lies at the root of God's act to transfer our allegiance to Christ. The atonement, as it transforms us, centers our lives around love.

> For the love of Christ leaves us no choice, when once we have reached the conclusion that one man died for all and therefore all mankind has died. His purpose in dying for all was that men, while still in life, should cease to live for themselves, and should live for him who for their sake died and was raised to life. With us therefore worldly standards have ceased to count in our estimate of any man; even if once they counted in our understanding of Christ, they do so now no longer. When anyone is united

to Christ, there is a new world; the old order has gone, and a new order has already begun (2 Cor. 5:14-17, NEB).

Love is what we experience in the example of Christ and just as God loved us in Christ, thereby setting things right; so, we too, motivated by love, set things right, struggle for justice. The New Testament is eloquent on this point as in the following passage from 1 John:

> Beloved, let us love one another; for love is of God, and he who loves is born of God and knows God. He who does not love does not know God; for God is love. In this the love of God was made manifest among us, that God sent his only Son into the world, so that we might live through him. In this is love, not that we loved God but that he loved us and sent his Son to be the expiation for our sins. Beloved, if God so loved us, we also ought to love one another (1 John 4:7-11).

Furthermore, certain passages in the New Testament make clear that the result of the atonement is not only our personal liberation from sin's bondage into the realm of the lordship of Jesus. This liberation is also marked by the appearance of a new social order which embodies the values of Jesus' teachings and life. As we have seen above, love and justice do not contradict each other. In fact, we discovered the opposite to be the case: love motivates shalom justice—indeed, love is expressed through this justice. As a result, just as God's love is expressed through Jesus as a power to establish justice and peace, so we who experience this love strive for a new community in which the old social divisions and the structures which maintain them no longer count. Thus, *the abolishment of all sinful relationships of oppression and exploitation is an essential part of why Christ died.*

That Jesus' death was to bring about a new social order realized through the formation of new relationships is clearly taught in Ephesians 2:14-17:

> For he is our peace, who has made us both one, and has broken down the dividing wall of hostility, by abolishing in his flesh the law of commandments and ordinances, that he might create in himself one new man in place of the two, so making peace and might reconcile us both to God in one body through the cross, thereby bringing the hostility to an end. And he came and preached peace to you who were far off and peace to those who were near.

The death of Christ was meant to bring about a reconciliation between enemies—here between Jews and Gentiles. This reconciliation was to be primary. Following this reconciliation, people in their new relationship were reconciled *together* to God. Note well the order of this passage. Reconciliation between peoples comes before reconciliation to God. We usually reverse this order. We think that reconciliation to God comes first, and then reconciliation to others is secondary and optional. Or we think that reconciliation to others is only possible after we are reconciled to God. Here we see that reconciliation to God comes after old enemies have made peace, becoming one, so that they together might be reconciled.

This theme is found again in Galatians 3:27-28, apparently an old baptismal formula. When people joined the church, affirming that they were in Christ, the old social distinctions and structures were no longer to count; Jew or Greek, slave or free, male or female.

The inward, subjective aspect of the atonement, and the outward social, objective aspect of the atonement are also connected in Colossians 3:10-11. Here the writer is exhorting Christians to live a Christian life—if we are raised with Christ, then we ought to have Jesus' values in mind. The author then gives examples of what this means, first, by stating what we are to leave off doing, and then what results from the new nature:

> . . . and have put on the new nature, which is being renewed in knowledge after the image of its creator. Here there cannot be Greek and Jew, circumcised and uncircumcised, barbarian, Scythian, slave, free man, but Christ is all, and in all.

The new nature which comes from our transformation, from the love of Christ controlling us, automatically results in a new way in human relations. Again, the old social divisions cannot any longer count among us. The New Testament does not here separate the personal aspects of the atonement—putting on the new nature and laying off the old—from the corporate aspects—the reconciliation of old enemies into one new society. To neglect either aspect of the atonement is to proclaim less than what Christ died to accomplish.

From these New Testament passages which describe what is to result from Jesus' death, we can see that it was understood to be a power transforming both people and society. Jesus' work is a positive work rather than mainly a negative one aimed at appeasing God or the devil. The spiritual and the social, the individual and the corporate are not divided into two separate spheres. Both new people and new structures are needed to bring about a new order which reflects shalom justice and in which people can experience shalom. In this regard, we must note that reconciliation does not take place in spite of sin and oppression, but because justice has taken place making things okay. *Our reconciliation to others, like God's reconciling work through Jesus, is based on and presupposes shalom justice; it is not whitewash.*

If the aim of the atonement is positive transformation toward shalom justice, then it cannot be separated from sanctification. Atonement and ethics go hand in hand. It is clear from the New Testament that the life and teachings of Jesus are to provide a model for us. There is no room here for oppression and injustice, domination, and repression. The opposite is, in fact, the case. We are liberated from the power of sin so that we might all be free, and being free so that we might serve one another. Romans 6 and Galatians 5:1-15 show that Christ frees and we are to remain free from all restraints so that we may serve.

Now, of course, it is clear that the church has not always or perhaps even very often struggled to remove the social divisions and structures which mar the human community. Insofar as this is the case, it would seem that the church has not embodied the power of the atonement. It might be that the church ought to begin the call to conversion with itself.

Atonement and shalom making

In light of the above, it would seem that those who have experienced the mind- and will-transforming power of the atonement are to be active workers for shalom—to make things okay in all aspects: materially, socially, and morally. We fulfill God's will for our lives when we respond to God's love in Jesus by becoming agents of shalom justice to bring about God's willed shalom on earth. *The struggle for shalom justice and okayness among people is the tangible evidence of the reality and the effectiveness of the atonement. To do less than this is to deny what God's act of justice in Jesus was understood to accomplish.*

But, in this work, we are opposed by the strong forces of evil, of sin, both individual sin and corporate, structural sin. The present age is an age of struggle between those who have been transformed and who are working for God's justice and shalom and those who block the way. This is a serious struggle because the battle is not only against flesh and blood, but against super-individual forces of evil embedded in nationalism, racism, classism, and sexism to name only a few of the demonic forces which block God's intentions for people on this earth.

We also know, that while the ultimate victory is on the side of those who work for God's justice and shalom, in the meanwhile the forces of repression and oppression often dominate. Rather than despair, the cross is the harbinger of hope that our struggle for God's shalom will one day bear fruit, if not in our life perhaps in the lifetime of our children or grandchildren. Impelled by this lively faith and hope, we as people transformed by God's love throw ourselves wholeheartedly into the struggle for shalom.

If the atonement is this transforming power, then should not the effects of the atonement become visible within the Christian church itself by eradicating all expressions of these demonic powers? If the message of the atonement is the good news, then should not Christian people be leading the way in modeling justice and shalom, as well as being agents bringing about justice and shalom for others? Is it not through the liberation from nationalism, classism, and sexism, and the presence of shalom in our lives that we sow the seeds of hope that indeed one day God's redemptive justice will triumph and there will be universal shalom? *Peacemaking as shalom making is making the power of the atonement real through new social relationships which reflect liberation from all forces which hold people in bondage.*

6. *Law: instrument for shalom justice*

N ow that we have looked at God's justice and its expression through salvation / liberation, we turn to the human side of the equation. What does it mean for people to be liberated?

This question can be divided into two parts. First, how should people respond to liberation? As we have seen, liberation must come before shalom, because it prepares the way for shalom. But, by itself, liberation does not produce shalom. So, how can liberated people build shalom?

Second, how do we maintain liberation? Once freed, how do we keep from slipping into oppression and exploitation? Yesterday's oppressed may become tomorrow's oppressors. How do those who have experienced God's salvation / liberation relate to others and form social structures that no longer oppress but liberate and lead to shalom?

In order to understand the link between God's acts of liberation and the human response to liberation, we will examine first a general pattern in the Bible which ties liberation and law together. From this pattern, we will be able to see the connection between God's work, liberation; and human response, law. Having seen this broader picture, we will examine how this pattern came to express itself as covenant. After placing the law in this framework, we will look at the purpose and work of biblical law, linking law with both justice and shalom.

The therefore pattern

In order to understand law as the responsible response to liberation, we must grasp a fundamental feature of biblical religion: law is found in the context of God's salvation. We tend to understand law and liberation as opposites: law represents one pole—legalism and limitation—while salvation or liberation represents the other—gift and freedom. However, in the Bible, law and liberation are closely connected.

Furthermore, the link between law and liberation is found in both testaments. Sometimes we separate the Bible into two opposite parts: the Old Testament which is law and the New Testament which is salvation and grace. However, as we shall see below, we find grace and liberation in both testaments and we find law in both testaments. Indeed, the linking together of liberation and law is a pattern connecting the two testaments.

Let's take the Ten Commandments to illustrate this pattern. These laws are regarded as the essence of biblical law. Here in short, clear statements are set forth the basic requirements of God for human life. In memorizing this passage, people usually begin with the first commandment, "You shall have no other gods before me" (Exod. 20:3). But this is not how the passage begins! It starts in verse 1 with "And God spoke all these words saying, 'I am Yahweh your God who brought you out of the land of Egypt, out of the house of bondage.' " First, there is a statement of God's grace: God's act of liberation. Based on what God has already done, the passage then continues: "[therefore] you shall have no other gods before me." The commandments spring from God's grace; they state how the people who have experienced liberation are now to respond.

This notion of the Ten Commandments as a response to liberation is further reinforced by the observation that they do not have penalty clauses attached to them. For example, the command prohibiting murder is not followed by any statement of what the penalty for murder is. This is a strange type of law! However, this law springs not from a concern for what will happen if you don't do it, but rather responds to what has already been done!

In Joshua 24, we find the farewell address of Joshua to the people of Israel. He begins his speech with a survey of their national history: how God led their ancestors, delivered them from Egypt, kept them safe in the wilderness, and, finally, gave them the good land of Palestine. Israel now holds all these things as a gift of God. Then, in verse 14, Joshua says, "Now therefore fear Yahweh and serve [God] in sincerity and in faithfulness; put away the gods which your [ancestors] served beyond the River, and in Egypt, and serve Yahweh." Here the *therefore* which links God's grace in the past with Israel's response in the present is clearly stated. What Israel is now expected to do is understood as a response to God's grace and liberation in the past.

In Psalm 105, this pattern occurs in a hymn praising God. This psalm begins with an invitation to praise God for all God's wonderful works for Israel. This litany of God's gracious acts toward Israel continues through verse 44. Then in the last verse of the psalm, verse 45, the psalmist concludes, "to the end that they should keep [God's] statutes, and observe [God's] laws. Praise Yahweh." The doing of the law is the fitting response to God's acts of grace.

Finally, consider several illustrations of this pattern in Deuteronomy. Look for example at how grace and law are chained together in Deuteronomy 10:12—11:12. Note the therefores in 11:1 and 11:8.

What God has done serves here as the basis of an exhortation to observe the law.

In Deuteronomy 26:1-11, we have the pattern in a different setting, a scene from worship. Here the Israelite peasants are commanded to offer up the firstfruits of their crop. They are to put them in a basket, bring them to the priest, and then say, "I declare this day to Yahweh your God that I have come into the land which Yahweh swore to our [ancestors] to give to us" (v.3). The priest will take the basket of firstfruits and place it before the altar. The worshiper now responds with a statement about what God has done for Israel in the past. The litany ends, with the statement, "And behold now I bring the first of the fruit of the ground which thou, O Yahweh, hast given me" (v.10). The offering of the firstfruits is a response to the gift of the land and God's help in time past. Worship here is understood as a response to God's grace: the bringing of the firstfruits was a response to God's gift of the land.

This pattern not only runs through the Hebrew Bible, but is also found in the Greek Scriptures. For example, in that well known verse, Romans 12:1, we find, "I appeal to you *therefore*. . . ." Paul has spent the first eleven chapters of the book on theological matters. He now turns to instruct Christians on how they should live. He prefaces these directions with *therefore* because the teachings which follow are a response to God's act of liberation in Jesus. Here again we see the same pattern, grace followed by law: what God has done followed by how people are now to live.

The same is found in Ephesians 4:1. Again, in the first three chapters of the book, the author sets out theology—what God has done through Jesus. Now in the last three chapters, we find instructions—how Christians are to live. These two sections of the book are connected like this: "I, therefore, a prisoner for the Lord, beg you to lead a life worthy of the calling to which you have been called." Here again *therefore* links theology and ethics, grace and human obedience. The instructions offered in chapters 4—6 are understood as a response to what we find in 1—3.

Again, we can see this pattern in 1 Peter 2:9ff. In verses 9 and 10, we find a series of statements describing God's grace toward Christian people, ending with "once you had not received mercy but now you have received mercy." Verse 11 follows with, "Beloved, I beseech you as aliens and exiles to abstain from the passions of the flesh. . . ." As a result of receiving mercy and now being God's people, the Christian is to respond to this mercy by living a proper life in response to this act of God.

Sometimes this pattern is described as the indicative followed by the imperative. That is, in the Bible, first, we find a telling of what God has done: the liberation which has taken place. This is the indicative. Then follows the command, the imperative, which instructs freed people on how to respond to their liberation.

Since this therefore pattern is found widely throughout the Bible and seems to reflect a fundamental conviction of biblical faith, it implies that we misunderstand the nature of God's grace when we remove it from the context of law. We misunderstand the meaning of law when we separate it from grace. In biblical religion, grace and law go together.

This fundamental insight of the Bible regarding law implies that biblical law is postliberation law. *Liberation is liberation from oppression not from law*. As a result, as we will see below, *biblical law was to be an instrument of shalom justice* and as such is a bulwark against oppression. This is in contrast to law as an instrument of distributive and retributive justice, where law tends to maintain inequalities. Distribution according to merit or based on having can protect the haves from the have-nots while retributive justice tends to mete out punishment to maintain the status quo, not to bring about a more just system. Biblical law is for people freed from the law of the oppressor!

Implications of the therefore pattern

Seeing law as grounded in and a response to God's grace has some important meanings for how we understand law and our obedience to it. In order to sharpen this point, we will contrast the mentality of legalism with that of obedience. This contrast we hope will also dispel a misunderstanding which equates the presence of law with legalism. Rather legalism and obedience are two different ways of understanding law. Legalism views law as imposed obligation; obedience is a response to divine grace and freedom.

First, obedience is a response to what God has already done, while legalism is doing right to gain a reward. Obedience recognizes that God's grace has already been given in the past; and, in the present, God continues to will the salvation of people from oppression. This basic will of God for history is a given fact and cannot be earned by any deeds on our part. What we do is a response to this given; we enter into action on this basis as co-workers with God. Thus, obedience understands law in the context of grace and history; it understand biblical law as a liberation instrument which, as we will see, is to realize, maintain, and promote shalom. Legalism, on the other hand, believes we must do what is right in order to earn God's favor or love. If we are good enough then God will reward us. Here, rather than responding to the divine will, we are working for wages.

In this differing perspective between obedience and legalism, it is a matter of balance and emphasis. Obedience can also look for a reward—the faithful workers should receive the wages or fruits of their

labor. In the Bible are ample promises of rewards for faithfulness—
Deuteronomy being a prime example. However, the reward for obedience is based on obedience as a response, rather than doing only for
the benefit of getting. For example, in the story of the three Hebrews
about to be thrown into the fiery furnace, they say,

> "O Nebuchadnezzar, we have no need to answer you in this
> matter. If it be so, our God whom we serve is able to deliver us
> from the burning fiery furnace; and he will deliver us out of your
> hand, O king. But if not, be it known to you, O king, that we will
> not serve your gods or worship the golden image which you
> have set up" (Dan. 3:16-18).

Here the three men express their loyalty and obedience to God
regardless of whether they are rewarded by immediate deliverance or
not. If God rewards them, good. We assume they would rather be
spared death in the furnace. But if they perish, they will still obey.

Second, obedience is liberating, because it is self-accepting; we do
not have to prove our self-worth before God, or before others. We
already have value because God loves us and has acted in grace toward
us. *God wills liberation for all; people do not have to earn the right to
be free*. Legalism, on the other hand, feeds on guilt and insecurity
because we can never quite be sure we are good enough or that our
efforts will suffice. As a result, legalism tends toward moralism and
contentions which can divert attention and energy from responding to
God's will for liberation and shalom.

Third, obedience is a response to God's grace here and now. We are
to be relevant to the moment and place in which we find ourselves. It
asks how can God's will for liberation and shalom be realized now in
this time and place? Legalism, however, looks toward the future where
the reward will be reaped. In order to gain its reward, it often mortgages
the present for the sake of the future. This can be seen in crass form in a
popular attitude toward morality—be good so you can go to heaven.
Tied to this notion of rewards being in the future is the idea that the
poor and oppressed ought to endure suffering now since they will get
their just rewards in heaven.

Covenant

Biblical faith, at certain points, formalized this therefore pattern by
understanding it as a covenant between God and the people. In the
concept of covenant, the biblical leaders took an originally secular
notion and used it to convey a theological insight.[1] In secular use, a

---

1. There is an extensive literature on the topic of covenant. I will list here some of the
sources which I have found helpful and have relied on in the following discussion.

covenant was an agreement made between two parties. The covenant defined their future relations. The keeping of these terms insured good relations.

In Genesis 26:26-31, we see such a covenant being made between Isaac and Abimelech. The result of this covenant was shalom, because they now had a relationship which was right.

An agreement could be contracted not only between individuals or groups but also between nations or other larger units. Joshua 9 presents an account of a covenantal agreement between Israel and the Gibeonites. Such political agreements we would normally call treaties in English. These agreements could be one sided, that is, one party could obligate the other. This is the case in Joshua 9:15, where the obligations seem to be entirely on the side of the Israelites. Or a covenant may be a way of obligating another, as in 2 Kings 11:4 where Jehoiada the priest put soldiers under a commitment which was sealed by making a covenant with them. Or there may be mutual obligations as in 1 Kings 5:12, where a treaty sealed terms between Solomon and Hiram, each of whom had obligations toward the other.[2]

The use of a covenant in order to regulate relationships and bring about shalom, as in the covenants mentioned, makes clear that relationships involve responsibility. When one enters into a relationship with another, it implies certain obligations to maintain and nourish the relationship. Otherwise a relationship could become one sided, exploitative and oppressive. When law is put in the context of covenant, the point of the law becomes in part to promote relationships which are okay.

On the part of God, the relationship with Israel began with care for Israel's ancestors, the rescue of Israel from slavery in Egypt, and finally the gift of the land. What now were Israel's obligations in the relationship? The covenant spells these out.

Another way to understand this point is to remember that God's love for the people was channeled through acts of liberation which expressed shalom justice. These initial acts of love by God set the basis for

Dennis J. McCarthy, *Treaty and Covenant: A Study in Form in the Ancient Oriental Documents and in the Old Testament*, second ed. (Rome: Biblical Institute Press, 1978); George E. Mendenhall, *Law and Covenant in Israel and the Ancient Near East*, in BA Reader 3(1970)3-53 (originally in *Biblical Archaeologist* 17(1954)24-46, 50-76); Moshe Weinfeld, *Deuteronomy and the Deuteronomic School* (Oxford: Clarendon Press, 1972); Dennis J. McCarthy, *Old Testament Covenant: A Survey of Current Opinions* (Oxford: 1972); E. Kutsch, "berit" *Theologisches Woerterbuch zum Alten Testament*; Moshe Weinfeld, "berit" *Theological Dictionary of the Old Testament*; D. N. Freedman, "Divine Commitment and Human Obligation," *Interpretation* 15(1964)419-31.

2. See Moshe Weinfeld's article, "berit," in *Theological Dictionary of the Old Testament* for a discussion of the various types of covenant in the Bible and their relationship to covenant and treaties in the Ancient Near East.

the relationship between Yahweh and Israel. The law, within the context of covenant and grace, now expresses how Israel channels its love toward God; how Israel enters into and maintains this shalom relationship established by God.

It seems significant that God enters into covenant with both a community and with individuals. However, the form of the covenant used is different. For individuals, a promissory covenant is used, as with Abraham in Genesis 15. In these, the emphasis is on what God will do and little is said about what the person is to do. For the community, an obligatory covenant is used as at Mount Sinai in the present form of the account in Exodus, which stresses the regulations or laws intended for the people. This type of covenant was set out to regulate the life of the community, God's people. This seems to imply that the law is the foundation of the community to which God wishes to relate. Or, said differently, the law is basic for a people who wish to be a liberated people, implementing shalom justice and experiencing shalom.

We have now seen how the covenant idea was used to describe the relationship between Yahweh and the people of Israel. How is this concept connected to the therefore pattern which we discussed at the beginning of this chapter? We began this section by saying that the therefore pattern was formalized through the use of covenant. How is this so?

First, as we have just seen, the covenant was a way of making clear the responsibilities involved in the relationship between God and people as assumed by the therefore pattern.

Second, the covenant pattern itself follows the therefore pattern. That is, in a covenant, the party making the covenant may tell what good things he has done. The following agreement then reflects how the covenant partners are to relate on the basis of this previous history. See for example the covenant in Genesis 26:26-31 which was made between Isaac and Abimelech. When Isaac asks why they have come, Abimelech replies, "We see plainly that Yahweh is with you; so we say, let there be an oath between you and us, and let us make a covenant with you, that you will do us no harm, just as we have not touched you and have done to you nothing but good and have sent you away in peace. You are now blessed of Yahweh" (vv. 28-29). Here the past history between them forms the basis for relationships between them. So also in covenants between God and people. As we have seen, the good things which God has done are mentioned first, and then the stipulations which will regulate their relationship follow.

Covenant in the New Testament

So far we have focused on the material in the Hebrew Bible, although we have tried to show how the therefore and covenant pattern permeate both sections of Scripture. Now, however, we will turn more deliberately to the New Testament to see how the term *covenant* is used there.

The Greek word for covenant is *diatheke*. It occurs thirty-three times in the New Testament; over half, seventeen, in Hebrews alone. The next most frequent user is Paul, with nine and then the Synoptic Gospels with four.

In the Synoptic Gospels, the term is used in reference to the death of Jesus. Luke 22:20 reads, "This cup which is poured out for you is the new covenant in my blood." Matthew has, "for this is my blood of the covenant, which is poured out for many for the forgiveness of sins" (Matt.26:28). Both of these passages rest on Mark 14:24. That the death of Jesus was the inauguration of a new covenant seems to be a well established early church tradition, since Paul, in 1 Corinthians 11:25 repeats, as a word which he has received from the Lord, "This cup is the new covenant in my blood. Do this, as often as you drink it, in remembrance of me."

Although *covenant* is not a frequent word, it is a most important one since it was selected to say what had happened in Jesus' death. Jesus was believed to have brought about a new covenant, a new day in the relationships between people and God and among people.

This notion that a new era has dawned in Jesus is also reflected elsewhere in the New Testament (literally, *new covenant*!). Paul uses the imagery of a new covenant to explain his role as minister in 2 Corinthians 3:6. Hebrews 9:15 speaks of Christ as the mediator of a new covenant. Although the word *covenant* itself is not used, probably the strongest statement in this regard is in Ephesians 3 where the author is explaining what has become new because of Jesus, which he refers to in verse 6 as the mystery of Christ: "that is, how the Gentiles are fellow heirs, members of the same body, and partakers of the promise in Christ Jesus through the gospel."

That is, the new covenant made through Jesus' death means that now the people of God have a new identity; the Gentiles, along with the Jews, received God's justice and liberating salvation. As a result of this covenant and new era, a new community was to be born, as noted in the previous chapter. (See Eph. 2:14-17; 2 Cor. 5:14-21.)

Implications of covenant for law

The immediate implication of covenant and the therefore pattern more generally is that since God was understood as the founder of the community through liberating work, all human ownership and lordship took second place. Indeed, oppressing and mistreating another person is an affront to God.

And since God gave them the land, it is God's and not theirs as Leviticus 25:23 says, ". . . the land is mine; for you are strangers and sojourners with me." Biblical covenant law thereby aims to decisively destroy all human feudalism in which people are in bondage to another. Covenant law is meant to free people from feudal structures and mentality. All are under God and none is privileged above another; all resources are for the good of the community, they are not for private exploitation at the expense of others.

The covenant form stresses the corporate and social dimension of being related to God. The people of God are a certain type of people; they form a certain type of community which is spelled out by the covenant. This implies strongly that to be in relationship with God is to form a special community which we can call the community of shalom.

The purpose of biblical law

So far, our conversation about the law has been in general terms. We have placed law in the context of grace and liberation and have explored its meaning from this aspect. But laws exist for a particular purpose—they are to bring about what a society considers to be good and proper. This is also the case in biblical law: the commands are given by God as an expression of what ought to be realized for the sake of all people.

What are these values or purposes which biblical law is to promote? We can answer this question from the laws themselves in two ways. First we can look at what are called the motive clauses.[3] Second we can examine the content of some of the laws to see what type of values and structures they would implement.

The motive clauses are a significant indicator for the aims of biblical law since they state the reasons or rationale for the law. These usually say that the law was given so that God's work of liberation and justice might be continued in the liberated community. For example, in Exodus 22:21, we find:

> You shall not wrong a stranger or oppress him, for you were strangers in the land of Egypt. You shall not afflict any widow or orphan. If you do afflict them, and they cry out to me, I will surely hear their cry; and my wrath will burn, and I will kill you with the sword, and your wives shall become widows and your children fatherless.

3. I have profited from Millard Lind's essay, "Law in the Old Testament," in *The Bible and Law*, ed. Willard Swartley, Occasional Papers 3 (Elkhart, Ind.: Council of Mennonite Seminaries, 1982), pp. 9-41.

Here the motive for keeping the law is both positive and negative: Israel has experienced liberation from oppression, so they are not to oppress. Likewise, they know that God frees the oppressed by bringing judgment on the oppressor so they can likewise expect judgment if they oppress. The law is both a stick and a carrot. Its motive clauses hold out the promise of justice and shalom for all if followed, and punishment if a people once liberated turn around and become oppressors. Here too we see the combination of a remembrance of the past (do, because of what has happened in the past) and a future consideration (reward or punishment), which we have noted above. In this case, future considerations are also based on past experience: you know what kind of God your God is.

Deuteronomy is especially rich in pointing to God's concern for the powerless and needy, and motivating the laws on the basis of Israel's own experience.

> For Yahweh your God is God of gods and Lord of lords, the great, the mighty, and the terrible God, who is not partial and takes no bribe. [Yahweh] executes justice for the fatherless and the widow, and loves the sojourner, giving him food and clothing. Love the sojourner therefore; for you were sojourners in the land of Egypt (10:17-19).

> You shall not pervert the justice due to the sojourner or to the fatherless, or take a widow's garment in pledge; but you shall remember that you were a slave in Egypt and the LORD your God redeemed you from there; therefore I command you to do this.

> When you reap your harvest in your field, and have forgotten a sheaf in the field, you shall not go back to get it; it shall be for the sojourner, the fatherless, and the widow; that the LORD your God may bless you in all the work of your hands. When you beat your olive trees, you shall not go over the boughs again; it shall be for the sojourner, the fatherless, and the widow. When you gather the grapes of your vineyard, you shall not glean it afterward; it shall be for the sojourner, the fatherless, and the widow. You shall remember that you were a slave in the land of Egypt; therefore I command you to do this (24:17-22).

It is clear from these passages that the motivation for the law was to keep the liberated community living as a community of the liberated ones.[4] The law continues this work of God. In this light, the law is a gift

---

4. These motive clauses are widespread in the law. See Exodus 23:9; Leviticus 19:33-36; 25:35-42; Deuteronomy 15:12-15; 16:12.

of God, just as the original act of salvation from Egypt was.

Second, the content of the laws is also significant and in line with these motivation clauses since many of the laws are concerned to meet the needs and protect the rights of the poor, needy, and weak. *By seeking justice for the needy, biblical law is an instrument for shalom.*

We can see this thrust of the law for liberating justice especially in the following types of commandments. First, there is the command to charity, as in Deuteronomy 14:28-29. These laws were aimed at providing for those who did not have access to the basic resources of the community. The local communities were to look out for their own poor and needy. The command to charity realizes that there will always be those in a community who do not have sufficient resources to meet their own needs. In our day we might add severely handicapped persons to this list.

Second, access to the product of the community was guaranteed to those who did not have ownership rights to the means of production. Here we have the gleaning laws quoted above in Deuteronomy 24:19-22. (See also Deut. 23:25-26 and Lev. 19:9-10.) Subsistence is not to be based on ownership, but on being a member of the community. Again, it will be the case that not everyone in a society will have means available for a livelihood, but will need to have access to the means of others. In these two laws, we can see that the problem is not with ownership, but with access to resources and how the product derived from them is distributed. There is to be equitable access and distribution.

Third, the law tackled the matter of access to the economic resources in the Sabbatical and Jubilee laws. These laws were a type of economic reform legislation to redistribute the capital resources of the community so that they would not become concentrated in the hands of a few. These laws are found in Exodus 23:11, Deuteronomy 15:1-11 and Leviticus 25. In these laws, two resources are to be redistributed: land and money. The result of this economic redistribution was to enable those who had lost out economically to once more regain their economic independence. This redistribution would also insure that great inequities in wealth and power would not grow up over time.

From these laws, we can see that biblical laws have a three-pronged approach to the problem of oppression and material inequality. The first was to care for those who could not care for themselves—sometimes charity is needed. Second, there are those who can manage but who need access on a regular basis—this too is provided for by the laws. Finally, there are those who could be productive and care for themselves if only they had control of some capital resource. For these, the laws mandated economic transformation, the redistribution of the capital goods.

The goal of the law as shalom justice, material well-being, just social relationships, and moral integrity, is also carried over into the New Testament in 2 Corinthians 8:8-14. Here Paul uses the example of Jesus who though he was rich became poor for us, to teach that those who have are to distribute to those who do not have in order to bring about equity. Here we are given the example of Jesus to motivate us.

The emphasis of the law on bringing about economic justice is further noted in the law's understanding of why people prosper, at least, in Deuteronomy. For example, Deuteronomy 15:10 points out that if we have and are asked, we are to give, for it is for this very reason that people prosper. Likewise, Deuteronomy 28:9-14 stresses that since a person's good fortune is due to God and not to their own cleverness or diligence alone, a person who prospers has an obligation to use that prosperity for economic justice.

From this short look at several of the laws coupled with our previous observations regarding the motive clauses, we can infer that the aim of the law is shalom justice. God has liberated and prospered the people so that they in turn might be a liberating people. Through the practice of these laws, justice will be expressed to the poor and needy and a community of shalom will result. The purpose of the law then is following liberation to create and regularize a set of new relationships, procedures, and structures which bring about shalom at the material, social, and spiritual level. The law is God's gift to people for the realization of shalom here and now.

Law and justice

The major implication of this chapter is that liberation in the Bible is not aimless. It is for something. Liberation's goal is embodied in the laws and teachings which are a response to and are motivated by liberation. These laws seek to maintain liberation by showing how a liberated community arranges its life.

This goal of biblical law to promote and maintain a liberated community so that there might be shalom should transform our understanding of law and justice. Laws, of course, do not apply themselves; people need to be willing and able to implement them. In this regard, we know that the structure of a society and its institutions govern day-to-day operation more than do abstract laws. Indeed, law can be seen as a reflection of these institutions and a guide to their operation. As a result, justice tends to become understood as procedure—justice results when the applicable law has been carried out. In this view of justice, laws become norms which in themselves determine whether justice is done. From this view of the law can arise the belief that following the law is the litmus test of justice. In this framework of thinking, the question of legality (is it legal? is it according to the law?) replaces the question of justice (is it right or just?).

In contrast to this procedural understanding of justice, shalom depends on justice understood substantively: justice is done when a just, okay state of affairs is the result. On this view, legality is not the test of justice, because laws themselves are unjust if they do not bring about a just result. Instead, the litmus test of justice is whether the powerless and oppressed receive aid and liberation so that there might be shalom. From this perspective, the prophets' use of the poor, the orphan, and the widow as an indicator of the presence or absence of justice makes sense.

These two different views of justice have significant consequences for the role of law in a society. When we understand justice procedurally, the law becomes a conservative force—it operates to maintain the status quo because it is primarily concerned with carrying out rules. When we understand justice as substantive, then law operates to transform society by instituting an equitable set of social relationships within the society. This latter function was, of course, the concern of biblical law. The implication of this seems to be that *only as justice passes this test, will it be shalom justice and lead to shalom. Shalom will not result from procedural justice alone.*

For those who have begun to experience God's liberation in their own lives and who align themselves with God's purposes in history, obedience to biblical law and teaching becomes a significant sign of commitment to liberation since it embodies a commitment to struggle for substantive justice.

This consideration may help explain the emphasis on obedience which permeates the Bible. For example, Jesus at the end of the Sermon on the Mount says:

> Not every one who says to me, "Lord, Lord," shall enter the kingdom of heaven, but [the one] who does the will of my Father who is in heaven. On that day many will say to me, "Lord, Lord, did we not prophesy in your name, and cast out demons in your name, and do many mighty works in your name?" And then will I declare to them, "I never knew you; depart from me, you evildoers" (Matt. 7:21- 23).

Here it seems clear that it is not the confessions which people make, but their obedience to the will of God which counts them as one of God's people. Even though they invoke the name of Jesus and do many mighty deeds, this does not authenticate them. Rather it is conformity to the will of God which signifies that one is a member of the kingdom of heaven.

Or again in 1 John 3:23-24:

> And this is his commandment, that we should believe in the
> name of his Son Jesus Christ and love one another, just as he has
> commanded us. All who keep his commandments abide in him,
> and he in them. And by this we know that he abides in us, by the
> Spirit which he has given us.
>
> And by this we may be sure that we know him, if we keep his
> commandments. He who says, "I know him" but disobeys his
> commandments is a liar; and the truth is not in him; but whoever
> keeps his word, in him truly love for God is perfected. By this we
> may be sure that we are in him: he who says he abides in him
> ought to walk in the same way in which he walked (2:3-6).

Thus even in the Johannine literature where belief plays such an
important part, this belief is manifested as obedience. That is, to believe
that God is sovereign is to obey the commandments which aims at
shalom justice. To reject the commandments is to reject shalom with
God and the struggle of the covenant community for liberation and
shalom now.

In light of this aspect of biblical law, why is the church not a more
positive force for the implementation of laws which make for shalom
justice? Why are Christian people so slow to change the laws which
work against the poor and powerless, the very people who are the test
which the Bible gives as to whether or not justice in fact is being done?

The implications of biblical law for shalom making seem clear. The
shalom maker is one who struggles for the carrying out of laws which
like biblical law are aimed at shalom justice. In this struggle, shalom
makers judge the morality of the law by how it benefits those who are
the litmus test of whether or not a law or policy is just: how does it help
the poor, oppressed, and powerless? On the other hand, the shalom
maker struggles against laws and policies which do not pass this test.

7. The state, shalom, and justice

T his is the first of three chapters in which we shall see how the core beliefs of biblical religion that we have just described were expressed in the life of Israel. Were these just pious convictions divorced from daily life or did these beliefs flow from and enter into the shaping of Israelite history and society?

In order to explore this dimension of biblical faith, we will turn to three moments in biblical history and thought: the rise of kingship and the state; the rise of what we call classical prophecy: Amos, Hosea, Micah, Isaiah, and others; and, finally, the life and teachings of Jesus as they center around these convictions.

We begin with the state because when we ask which institution in a society is most responsible for how the law is applied, the type of justice done, and the general well-being of people, we think of the state. In ancient Israel, this meant kingship, for that was the form of the state which Israel had. We will look first at the rise of kingship in Israel. Why did Israel adopt kingship and how did this new institution affect its society? Second, we will examine the background of kingship in the ancient Near East and in Israel: what was kingship supposed to do and how was it to work?

The rise of kingship in Israel

As is well known, kingship was not native to Israel. It borrowed it from its neighbors at a particular point in its history (1 Sam. 8). Israel existed before the state and lived on after the state; its existence did not depend on the state. Thus, for Israel, the state was not a given, but was chosen.

Why did Israel borrow this foreign institution? What did it stand to gain and to lose from having a state? And perhaps even more important, what happened to Israelite society as the result of taking on this institution?

In order to answer these questions, we need to take a brief look at Israel's history: what was Israel like before the state, and what was it like after the state? From these before and after snapshots of its society, we can understand why Israel chose to have a king and what happened to Israel as a result of this choice. Knowing this, we will be able to see what the state has to do with shalom and the making of shalom justice through law.

Israel before it had a king

Since the rise of kingship is reported in 1 Samuel, we need to go the Book of Judges to discover what Israel was like before the state. In this book, we have a series of stories about war heroes who delivered Israel from its enemies in time of need. The enemies against whom these leaders fought, with one exception, were neighboring peoples who entered Israelite territory and oppressed them. These leaders were thus called saviors or deliverers, because they liberated the people from oppression.

In looking at the stories of these deliverers, we get glimpses into the Israelite society of that time. The information is fragmentary, but drawing on these clues, we can paint a brief picture of the main features of this society.

The first striking feature in these stories is that words for flocks or herds are rare—Judges 5:16, in describing the tribes living across the Jordan River, being an exception. (See also Judg. 18:21 for a note on Dan.) Elsewhere the people are seen cultivating the soil, growing grain and grapes. Meat is rarely eaten; in fact, it seems reserved for special occasions and sacrifices (Judg. 6:19; 13:15, 19; 15:1). The people work their fields during the day, returning to the village at nightfall (Judg. 13:9; 19:16). It seems then that Israel in this period was mainly composed of farmers settled in scattered unwalled villages. These villages were near to the fields and it was mostly those who worked in the fields who lived here.

People lived in extended families called "father's house" (*beth ab*) which could consist of several dwellings or "houses" (Judg. 18:14, 22). Here lived the father, the adult sons, their wives and servants (Judg. 6:30). This was the smallest unit of legal responsibility and liability; the 'house of the father' was held responsible in some sense for what its members did (Judg. 6:30; 8:35; 9:16, 19). They also were responsible for the burial of family members (Judg. 16:31). This extended family appears to have been the basic economic unit; it was both the unit of production and consumption.

Above this basic social group, was the clan, or "family" (*mishpachah*). Members of a clan might live together in a village (Judg. 6:24; 8:32). It consisted of a number of father's houses (9:5). The clans, in turn, belonged to tribes. What is striking in Judges is that, apart from the last chapters (18—21) which do not tell of deliverers, the word for tribe (*shebet*) does not appear. Moreover, within the individual stories of the deliverers (Judg. 3—16), all twelve tribes never act together.[1]

Usually a union of several tribes is formed, for a short period, under the leadership of a single person to repel an invading enemy (4:6, 10; 6:35). The picture we get of group life in general is much the same as that of life in the villages: decentralized and under local control. Rarely were larger groups formed beyond the village level, and these only in extreme cases for defense against outside oppressors.

The political organization mirrors this picture of the social structure. The elders were the main figures who, we assume, ran things on a day-to-day basis. However, in time of war, *sarim* (lieutenants) organized the troops and led them into battle. The lieutenants themselves were under the command of an overall leader, sometimes called a *qatsin* or general.

The story of Jephthah (Judg. 10:17—11:11) illustrates this structure and the organization of civil and military leadership. In 10:18, the *sarim* seek someone to lead them into battle with the Ammonites. This person, they say, will be their *rosh* (head). But no one can be found for this function, so it is up to the elders to find someone. They approach Jephthah, and at first offer him the title of *qatsin*, but he refuses. Then they offer him both *qatsin* and *rosh*, both generalship and headship. The latter evidently was an office which extended beyond the time of military action. This Jephthah accepts. The elders then bring him to the people: they accept him, and Jephthah becomes both general and head.

From this episode, we note two aspects of political organization. First, strong overall leadership was not in place during normal times; someone had to be selected in time of emergency to meet the crises. Evidently, such military leadership lasted as long as the crisis, unless the person was also ratified as head. Second, there was a dual structure; there were the local leaders for civil affairs, the elders, and there were the local leaders for fighting, the lieutenants. It was up to the elders to make the political arrangements and up to the lieutenants to take care of organizing the people for fighting.[2]

---

1. Scholars usually make a distinction between the original narratives about the deliverers and later editorial material which now links these stories together and places them in an all Israelite context. The point here is that within the actual stories there is no united Israel, only tribal coalitions. It is in the editorial material that Israel as a whole is depicted.

2. This picture fits the observations of Lucy Mair, *Primitive Government* (Baltimore: Penguin Books, 1962), regarding tribes without government: "Between the close-knit hunting band and the organization of the state type there is a form of polity characteristic of populations which are a good deal larger than the hunting band, though not necessarily smaller than those which are governed as states . . . one could say that some populations regard themselves, and are regarded by others, as distinct entities, but yet do not recognize any person or body of persons as having general authority to take decisions in matters affecting them all" (p. 106). This description seems to fit Israel in the time of the Judges. Two political features are typical of these social groups: (1) There is generally a

In short, what we see of Israel in the stories of the deliverers is a decentralized group of rural cultivators organized along kinship and family lines. They had no permanent central institutions as far as we can see. Alliances are fluid and temporary, called into being under pressure from outside forces. We might call this type of society a ranking society. Everyone in a given class has equal access to the economic resources of the community. Some may gather more wealth or more prestige, but all have equal access to resources for their own livelihood.[3]

Israel under the monarchy

With the rise of the monarchy, we see the emergence of a different type of society, with different structures and institutions. To be sure, most of the people remain rural cultivators, but they operate now within a different social framework; they become peasants, part of a larger centralized social order. We find the story of the rise and development of the monarchy in 1 and 2 Samuel and the first twelve chapters of 1 Kings. What happened to Israel in this transition?

Of course, the forms of social life which we found during the period of the Judges continue. The father's house is still the basic social unit, which is still headed by elders (2 Sam. 12:17). The clan is active at the beginning of this period, seeking blood vengeance (2 Sam. 14:7) and performing religious rites (1 Sam. 20:6).

But new factors are at work in Israelite society in a powerful way. First, a move toward urban life is under way. Israelites are now living in walled cities which are evidently small urban centers (1 Sam. 6:18; 7:14; 30:27-31). Also, the widespread development of terracing in the Israelite hill country probably goes back to this time.[4] This implies increased capital investment in the means of production (land) and the possibility for greater yields as well as the growing of grain in the hill

distinction between elders, the political leaders, and warriors, those who take leadership in war. (2) Pan-tribal leaders are religious but without any force available to make people obey them. These two features certainly seem to characterize Israel in the pre-state period. (Samuel would be an example of the latter point, a pan-tribal religious leader.)

3. The understanding of the dynamics of Israelite society is aided by cooperative works in anthropology and sociology which have studied how certain social, economic, and political features and systems cluster together, so that, given a certain economic system, one can fill in what were the likely social and political dynamics. For examples of this type of analysis, see: Elman R. Service, *Primitive Social Organization: An Evolutionary Perspective* (New York: Random House, 1962); Morton H. Fried, *The Evolution of Political Society: An Essay in Political Anthropology* (New York: Random House, 1967); Gerhard Lenski and Jean Lenski, *Human Societies: An Introduction to Macrosociology* 4th ed. (New York: McGraw-Hill, 1982).

4. See C.H.J. de Geus, "The Importance of Archaeological Research into the Palestinian Agricultural Terraces, with an Excursus on the Hebrew Word *gbi*^*," *Palestine Exploration Quarterly* 107(1975)65-74.

country. This is coupled with the possibility of increased productivity due to the use of the plow and of iron (1 Sam. 8:12; 13:20), neither of which is mentioned in Judges. This promise of greater production increases the ability of the peasants to produce a surplus and support an urban population.[5]

Second, and most important, is the rise of centralized government: the state with its supporting institutions and personnel. The new features which come with the state can be grouped under three headings. First are the group of men who support the king in running and maintaining his throne and kingdom. This support personnel consists of the experts who make up the state bureaucracy, the members of the cabinet, and their helpers (1 Sam. 18:5, 22-24; 2 Sam. 8:16-17; 20:25-26). Here we see a group of people whose loyalty is to the king and state rather than to local kinship groups. It is convenient for the rise of the state to have those whose ties and loyalties are to the central government rather than to local and regional interests. Otherwise local interest would checkmate the plans of the state.[6]

A second feature associated with the rise of the state is militarization. We see the rise not only of the Israelite military elite like Joab, but also the presence of elite, foreign mercenary troops on whose support the king relied to maintain his power. Two incidents vividly portray how the balance of power came to lie in the hands of these state troops.

First, in the rebellion of Absalom against David, the popular army (that is, the militia) was behind Absalom. David was left with his 600 professional soldiers (2 Sam. 15:18). With their support, David defeated the Israelite militia and regained his throne. Following this defeat, the popular army fades from history.[7] Power is now concentrated in the hands of the professional military under control of the king.

---

5. See the trenchant comment of Charles L. Redman, *The Rise of Civilization: From Early Farmers to Urban Society in the Ancient Near East* (San Francisco: W. H. Freeman, 1978): "Urban societies . . . are developed through intense specialization of tasks and great inequalities in the distribution of wealth. Fundamental for these two processes was the availability of surplus wealth that could be invested in specialized activities and that supported the wealthier classes" (p. 321). This meant that redistribution needed to be controlled in such a way that it would result in wealth differentiation rather than in equality. It has been noted that generally intensification of production precedes the rise of states making the possibility of a surplus available for support of the state and the ruling elite. See Henry T. Wright, "Recent Research on the Origin of the State," *Annual Review of Anthropology* 6(1977)379-97.

6. As Mair comments, one of the two important factors for the rise of kingship was the ability to attract and retain a group of persons upon whom the king could count and who identified more closely with the king than with the people. See *Primitive Government*, p. 108.

7. For the demise of the popular militia, see Haim Tadmor, "The People and the Kingship in the Biblical Period," in *Jewish Society Through the Ages*, ed. H. H. Ben-Sasson and S. Ettinger (London: Vallentine Books, 1971), pp. 46-68.

The second incident is the coronation of Solomon. Solomon's brother Adonijah was supported by several powerful figures, Joab and Abiathar, but in the end Solomon won out supported by the professional troops (1 Kings 1).

Along with the rise of the elite at court, both civilian and military, the size of the standing army and the level of military technology increase greatly. This is seen in the rise of chariot forces in Israel's army. In the early days, David had no need for horses, because Israel had no chariots. So when David captured horses, he hamstrung them (2 Sam. 8:4). However, by Solomon's time, things were different! We read of 40,000 stalls for horses and 12,000 horsemen (1 Kings 4:26; 10:26).[8] This change had dramatic meaning for Israel. First of all, the horses and men needed to be fed, so some kind of taxation was needed to support the military establishment. And second, the charioteers were trained professionals; they were full-time warriors in contrast to the popular militia which fought during the period of the Judges and the early monarchy.

This dependency on a standing army shows again a shift in Israelite governance from one in which authority is with the people to one in which it rests with centralized powers. Before, leaders led by virtue of widespread popular support which to some extent was based on what the leader did to benefit the people. (Note, in Jephthah's case, his headship depended on delivering the people from oppression.) Now authority rests on force, the ability to use military might, and the leader benefits from the surplus of the people.

This leads us directly to the third essential feature of the state: the need to accrue and concentrate a surplus in order to support the central government and the forces upon which it depends.[9] This came about in two major ways. First, the state taxed the people. We read about two types of taxation. The one is corvée, where people are forced to work for a certain part of the year on state projects (1 Kings 4:27-28).

Second, there was taxation in kind, either in foodstuff or in precious materials which were needed by the elite at court. First Kings 4:7-19 and 5:6-8 refer to the division of Israel into twelve districts, and each one provided the court with food for a month. A chief overseer was

---

8. For a discussion of Hebrew *parash* with a conclusion that here it means *mares* see D.R. Ap-Thomas, "A King's Horses: A Study of the Term PRSH (1 Kings 5:6[EVV., 4:26]).

9. The acquiring of surplus was necessary for the rise of the state because the king had to pay those who were loyal to him and supported his kingship as over against the centripetal forces of tribalism and local autonomy. See Mair, *Primitive Government*: "We begin to see already how important it is for the building up of kingship that the society should have some surplus of wealth which can be concentrated in the hands of the ruler and used for purposes of state—among which one of the most important is rewarding services" (p. 109).

responsible to coordinate the work of the governors who were over the districts.[10]

Beyond taxation, which was the accrual of product, capital resources (land) were redistributed and concentrated in the hands of the ruling and urban elite. This was done, at least, in the beginning, through the development of prebendal estates. These were landed estates given to high officials at court. The produce from them was used for their support. See 1 Samuel 8:14 for a warning about this development; in 1 Samuel 22:7 it already seems to be a reality under Saul, who fears that David is offering his men even greater estates than he has given them. Under David, we can see it in operation. In 2 Samuel 9:9-10, David confers the right to land on Mephibosheth. His servant Ziba, along with his fifteen sons and twenty servants, is to work the land and bring the produce to Mephibosheth for his support in Jerusalem. (Other references to land owned by court figures are in 2 Sam. 13:23; 14:30; 1 Kings 2:26.)

This notion of the land as a resource of production for the support of someone who did not live on the land but profited from the work of others changed Israelite attitudes toward the land. It became a commodity and title could be readily transferred by the king. In 2 Samuel 16:4 and 19:30, we see David transferring rights to estates. The effect of this practice was to concentrate ownership of resources in fewer hands and to pump produce from the land into the urban centers.

The result of this centralization was, of course, that in Jerusalem and probably in other urban centers as well, the elite became wealthy and enjoyed a lavish lifestyle. See the description of Solomon's court in 1 Kings 4:22-24; in 10:27, it says that Solomon made silver in Jerusalem like stones. All of this prosperity came from somewhere. Some came from trade, some from tribute, but much of it was from the work of the rural Israelites who were no longer free rural cultivators but peasants, part of a state network.

We can see, in light of these findings, the tremendous shift in the structure and function of Israelite society from the period of the judges to that of the kings. From a ranking society, where everyone had equal access to basic resources, it shifted to a stratified one, where the urban elite in Jerusalem and perhaps in other cities enjoyed a way of life far beyond that possible for the people working the land in their rural villages. Thus emerged the possibility and actuality of poverty and

---

10. This taxation under Solomon evidently reached unbearable proportions, leading to the the revolt of the northern tribes immediately after his death. A student of mine, Mr. James Milligan, estimated that under kingship a rural farming family went from having a surplus of almost fourteen bushels of grain a year to having a grain deficit. This was estimated on how much grain it would take to feed Solomon's chariot force and how much labor would be lost due to corvée work on state projects.

affluence existing side by side. The following chart is an attempt to show some of these shifts more clearly.

Shift from kinship governance to state

Prestate	State
Rank depends on popular support; generosity, redistribution	Rank depends on inherited status; accrual of surplus; concentration
Leadership emerges and depends on popular support	Body of paid retainers allows state to escape popular checks and balances
Kin group officials; local	Bureaucracy; national
Organization along family kinship lines	Political territorial organization
Social solidarity; equality in living styles	Extravagant living for king and elite
Private, domestic architecture	Monumental, state building needing massive labor inputs
Local groups furnish warriors; military leaders chosen as needed	State army in place under permanent leadership

This shift raises a question: Why would anyone want to change from being a free rural cultivator to a peasant? Why would the Israelites choose to bear the burden of kingship? To understand this choice, we turn now to the forces which led Israel to choose a king.

Why the shift to kingship?

First, there was the factor of natural social change. As we have just seen, in the period of the deliverers, Israel was made up of rural cultivators living in small agricultural villages. The society was highly decentralized, with people living in extended families.

When we reach the period of the rise of kingship, the situation was changing. Population density was increasing. Iron farm implements came into use, making larger harvests possible. It seems that terracing in the hill country of Israel was becoming more extensive. This shows, as suggested above, capital investment, greater productivity, and the growing of grain in the hill region.

As a result of these changes in production, Israelite society was becoming more complex. An urban culture was emerging. The rise of a priestly order and prophets showed that vocations were becoming more specialized. And, finally, the gap between rich and poor was growing wider. The contrast between Nabal, the rich herder (1 Sam. 25:2-13) and the men who gathered around David, "every one who was in distress, and every one who was in debt, and every one who was discontented gathered to him; and he became captain over them" (1 Sam. 22:2) is clear. The natural social change from a decentralized, rural, farming people to a more urbanized, specialized, and economically stratified society had begun and was beginning to take its social toll.

In this context, we can understand Nabal's answer to David's men when they asked for protection money: "Who is David? Who is the son of Jesse? There are many servants nowadays who are breaking away from their masters" (1 Sam. 25:10). The increasing complexity of the society, its increasing specialization and wealth differentiation led to law and order problems.

This leads us to the second factor which lies behind the rise of kingship: the breakdown of the traditional form of internal governance. This is the primary reason given in 1 Samuel 8 for the people's request for a king. The sons of Samuel, whom he had installed as judges, "perverted justice." Thus the clan leaders, the elders, got together and asked for a new form of leadership; the old model did not seem to be working.

The failure of the old system is also the theme of the two stories which are added on to the deliverer stories in the Book of Judges. In 17:6, we find the phrase, "In those days there was no king in Israel; every man did what was right in his own eyes." This phrase is found again in 18:1 and again, in part, in 19:1. It also provides the conclusion to the Book of Judges in 21:25. The intent seems clear; internal chaos reigned because there was no king. Rule by might leads to the violation of social norms, the oppression of the weak and, finally, the tribe of Benjamin is nearly wiped out. The old governance system was no longer adequate for Israel's new social situation.

Finally, there was the Philistine menace. The people not only ask for a king who will govern them but also one who will, "go out before us and fight our battles" (1 Sam. 8:20). They wanted a military leader who could lead them to success in their struggle with the Philistines for control of Palestine.

With increasing social complexity, inner social tensions, and outside military threats, a new form of governance seemed necessary. Real dangers and needs seemed to justify the people's call for a king. But as we have seen above, regardless of whatever benefits people hoped to reap as a result of kingship, they also received burdens to be borne. Why did Israel choose and continue kingship in spite of these burdens? In fact, in 1 Samuel 8, Samuel is shown warning the people ahead of time that if they choose to have a king, the king will oppress them. What view of kingship did people have which led them to view it in a positive light in spite of these warnings and the burdens that followed?

In order to explore this question, we need to look at the ideas about the function and purpose of kingship which went with the institution. Since kingship was borrowed, in order to examine the thinking about kingship in Israel we will begin with how kingship was viewed by those from whom Israel was borrowing it. In this probe of kingship, we will limit ourselves primarily to the notion that the king was to uphold the law and maintain justice because this is the focal point of our interest in the state. Also, for the sake of brevity, we will look only at kingship in Mesopotamia since its ideology seems to have been the most influential on Israel.[11]

Kingship in the Ancient Near East

In Mesopotamia, unlike in Israel, kingship was an institution of divine origin. We read in the "Sumerian Kinglist": "When kingship was lowered from heaven. . . ." (Pritchard, *Ancient Near Eastern Texts*, p. 265) or in the Sumerian flood story, "After the lofty crown and the throne of kingship had come down from heaven. . . ."[12] Kingship was something given for the benefit of humankind; it was part of the process of civilization.

Not only was the institution itself of heavenly origin, but the kings themselves were said to have been called by the gods to the throne. For example,

> But when Ningirsu, the foremost warrior of Enlil, gave the kingship of Lagash to Urukagina, and his hand had grasped him out of the multitude; then he (Ningirsu) enjoined upon him the (divine) decrees of former days.

> When An and Enlil had called Lipit-Ishtar, the wise shepherd . . . to the princeship of the land in order to establish justice in the

11. For a recent survey of Israelite kingship ideology in relationship to Ancient Near Eastern royal ideology, see Moshe Weinfeld, "Zion and Jerusalem as Religious and Political Capital: Ideology and Utopia," in *The Poet and the Historian: Essays in Literary and Historical Biblical Criticism*, ed. Richard E. Friedman (Scholars Press: Chico, Calif., 1983), pp. 75-115.

12. Found in Lambert and Millard, *Atra-hasis*, translated by M. Civil, p. 141.

land, to banish complaints, to turn back enmity and rebellion by force of arms, and to bring well-being to the Sumerians and Akkadians. . . .[13]

The call by the gods to be king was for a purpose: to institute justice for the people of the land so that there might be well-being. In the first quote above, the text goes on to mention reforms which Urukagina brought about in order to restore justice. Likewise, in the case of Lipit-Ishtar, he brought justice to the land through concrete actions which are mentioned later in the text. And Hammurabi's famous law collection referred to justice as the proper exercise of kingship.

> When the exalted Anu . . . called me by name Hammurabi . . . to make justice appear in the land, to destroy the evil and the wicked that the strong might not oppress the weak. . . .

> When Marduk commanded me to give justice to the people of the land and to let (them) have (good) governance, I set forth truth and justice throughout the land (and) prospered the people.

> That the strong may not oppress the weak (and) so to give justice to the orphan and the widow I have inscribed my precious words on my monument . . . to judge the judgment of the land (and) decide the decision of the land (and) so to give justice to the oppressed.[14]

Thus we see that the king was expected to maintain justice in the land for the good of the citizens because this was part of the proper work of kings. This justice was seen when the strong did not oppress the weak, when the underclasses were protected and given justice. How did the king go about ensuring that this type of justice was done?

The king promoted this justice in three main ways. One was by the publishing of law collections, like those of Hammurabi. However, this seemingly had little if anything to do with the actual practice of law in everyday life. The law codes apparently were more a testament to the good intentions and wisdom of the king than a guide to the actual practice of law. Second, the king could decide individual cases brought to him by the people. This they did, and the king or his officials were

13. S. N. Kramer, *The Sumerians: Their History, Culture, and Character* (Chicago: University of Chicago Press, 1963); the first quote is from Urukagina of Lagash, p. 317, the second is from the "Lipit-Ishtar law code," p. 336.

14. G. R. Driver and John C. Miles, *The Babylonian Laws* (Oxford: Clarendon Press, 1955), vol. 2, pp. 7, 13 from the prologue to the laws and p. 97 from the epilogue.

called upon to make many decisions. Third, the king could institute economic and social reforms which were designed to correct injustices and inequities which had come about in the society. The most famous and extensively preserved of these reforms is that of Ammi-Saduqa.[15] In these reforms, prices were fixed, tariffs set, land returned to previous owners, slaves released; it was a general readjustment of the society toward a more just order.

The words used to describe justice in the law codes and reform texts are usually *kittum u mesharum*. *Kittum* seems to designate the right or proper order that ought to exist, while *mesharum* refers to the just carrying out of this proper order. They are used together to show the entire scope of justice—right norms being properly implemented. Thus the reform act of Ammi-Saduqa is to establish *mesharum* again, that is to bring about a more fair society.

We can see from this scanty survey that the proper function of kingship is to maintain the proper order through just procedures. Order is proper when the people are protected from outside aggressors and from internal oppressors. It is maintaining an order which liberates, where the weak and dispossessed are not taken advantage of nor enslaved by the powerful and advantaged. This is a powerful vision of real justice that kept on working, and we can understand why it would be an attractive one to Israel in the situation in which it chose kingship.

Kingship in Israel

It is not surprising then that this understanding of kingship is also found in Israel. Here too the king was responsible to bring about and maintain a just order. In exercising this charge, the king mirrored the justice of God, who was sovereign over all the universe. Psalm 72 is particularly clear in this regard.[16]

> Give the king thy justice, O God,
> and thy righteousness to the royal son!
> May he judge thy people with righteousness,
> and thy poor with justice!
> Let the mountains bear prosperity [shalom!] for the people,
> and the hills, in righteousness!
> May he defend the cause of the poor of the people,
> give deliverance to the needy,
> and crush the oppressor! (vv.1-4).

15. F. R. Kraus, *Ein Edikt des Konigs Ammi-Saduqa von Babylon* (Leiden: E. J. Brill, 1958).

16. For the close parallelism of ideas and even phraseology of this psalm to royal ideology in the Ancient Near East see Weinfeld, "Zion and Jerusalem," pp. 93ff.

For he delivers the needy when he calls,
the poor and him who has no helper.
He has pity on the weak and the needy,
and saves the lives of the needy.
From oppression and violence he redeems their life;
and precious is their blood in his sight (vv.12-14).

The king is responsible for justice and righteousness on earth. In doing this, he reflects the will of God for justice and shalom in human society. The two Hebrew words here, *mishpat* (justice) and *tsedaqah* (righteousness) taken together, like the Akkadian words *kittum u mesharum*, indicate what justice is about—the proper implementation of just norms in the society. Righteousness, *tsedaqah*, is the proper order, while justice, *mishpat*, is doing justice to achieve the just order which results in shalom. Seen this way, justice, to be true justice must be both substantive—bring about a right order in the society—and procedural, it must bring about this right end through fair and equitable means. Thus the basic fundamental principle of the state was to be concerned with the right ordering of society which would bring the experience of shalom to the people. In this, it was to reflect God's justice and concern for humankind.

Just as justice was basic to God's rule, so was it also for the human king. Justice was the foundation of his throne; the survival of his rule depended on it. We find these sentiments captured in pragmatic advice found in Proverbs.

It is an abomination to kings to do evil, for the throne is established by righteousness (Prov. 16:12).

By justice a king gives stability to the land, but one who exacts gifts ruins it (Prov. 29:4).

If the king judges the poor with equity his throne will be established for ever (Prov. 29:14).

Doing justice was basic to kingship. That it was a necessary part of being a legitimate king was not just rhetoric as we can see from 2 Samuel 15:1ff, which depicts the beginning of Absalom's revolt. Absalom would arise early in the morning and stand by the gate of the city of Jerusalem. Now the gate was the place of justice, so he would be standing on the steps of the supreme court building, so to speak. As people would come for justice, he would call them aside, ask them who they were and what was their complaint. They would explain their case to him. After hearing them out, Absalom would reply that it looked like they had a good case; but, alas, there was no one present from the king to give them justice. Then he would add that he wished he were king, for if he were, he would give the people justice. Absalom's strategy was successful. Israel rallied to him and his revolt.

How was the king, David, supposed to implement justice and righteousness for the people? We can mention two ways. First, by having a proper court system where the cases of all were heard and decided fairly, so that the weak would not be oppressed by the powerful. This David did not seem to be doing.

Secondly, the king was to implement reform to bring the society back into balance, to make the situation just. Since in the Bible all laws are presented as given by God to the covenant people, the king provided for substantive justice by seeing that these laws were implemented and justice done. As we saw in the chapter on the law, biblical law implemented substantive justice and shalom in three ways.

First are laws enjoining charity and sharing with the needy, the weak, and the powerless. An illustration of this type of law is Deuteronomy 14:28-29, where the tithe of the third year is to go in its entirety to meet the needs of those in the local community who do not have access to the land, the basic capital resource of the community. Note also the laws in chapter 16 which enjoin sharing sacrificial and festival meals with these same classes. The king was to promote an equitable redistribution of product rather than to support its concentration.

Second, there are laws granting access rights to resources. This is to enable those who do not have land to have a share in the produce of the land. The gleaning laws illustrate this type of law. (See Lev. 19:9-10; Deut. 23:24-25; 24:19-22.) The state was to promote open access to livelihood resources.

Third are the reform laws which redistribute the capital resources so that more people may enjoy their use. These are the sabbatical year laws in Exodus 23:11; Deuteronomy 15:1-11 and Leviticus 25. The state was to correct an imbalance in the accumulation of capital resources, so that some may not concentrate ownership of resources in their hands while others have none. These provisions we have seen above are paralleled by reforms which were proclaimed by Mesopotamian kings.

All these laws, as mentioned previously, were aimed at implementing shalom justice—the flow of resources from those who have to those who are in need. Thereby substantive justice was brought about, things were as they should be and shalom experienced.

Thus in the ideology of kingship in Israel as it is related to justice and shalom, the responsibility of the king was to meet the needs of the people by seeing that substantive justice was a reality in the land. By this action, the justice of the state mirrored divine justice. This mirroring is assumed not only by Psalm 72, discussed above, but also by Psalm 89, in which God's justice is directly connected with the king's justice. Again, a comparison of Psalm 72 with Psalms 82 and 146, which illustrate God's justice, will show the further parallelism of God's and the king's justice. Both are focused on substantive justice for the poor, weak, and oppressed. This is the litmus test for justice which leads to shalom.

Ideology and reality

Given this understanding of the function of the king and of the state, we can appreciate how in a situation of anarchy, increasing oppression and the concentration of wealth, not to mention the imminent threat of foreign oppression, the people might well cry out for a king. However, there were dangers as well. The king and the state might not serve the oppressed, but themselves and their powerful allies. The people were warned about this by Samuel (1 Sam. 8:11-18). The king instead of being a liberator and a power for justice could become an oppressor.

Thus the fate of Israel, the liberated people of God, hung in the balance. Would the the king maintain their liberation against the rising forces of oppression and anarchy where the stronger oppressed the weak? Would the king promote substantive justice measured by the defense of the rights of the weak, by aid to those in distress, and by crushing the power of the oppressors?

As we shall see in the next chapter, the prophets declared that reality did not match vision. The state, in fact, was not providing substantive justice which led to liberation and shalom. Rather, the state was on the side of the oppressors.

The New Testament view of the state

We do not have space here to discuss the New Testament view of the state, except to say that it is in line with what we have discovered about the state and kingship in the Hebrew Bible.[17] That is, the state does have a legitimate function: it is to do good and promote substantive justice and can be appealed to on this basis. But, as a matter of fact, it often does not do this. In cases where states do not carry out justice, they stand under God's judgment, as all evildoers and oppressors do. This is eloquently expressed in the Wisdom of Solomon:

> Hear then, you kings, take this to heart; learn your lesson, lords of the wide world; lend your ears, you rulers of the multitude, whose pride is in the myriads of your people. It is the Lord who gave you your authority; your power comes from the Most High.

---

17. See my discussion of Romans 13:1-7 in *From Word to Life* (Scottdale, Pa.: Herald Press, 1982), pp. 166-72, and bibliography cited there.

He will put your actions to the test and scrutinize your intentions. Though you are viceroys of his kingly power, you have not been upright judges; you do not stand up for the law or guide your steps by the will of God. Swiftly and terribly will he descend upon you, for judgement falls relentlessly upon those in high place. The small man may find pity and forgiveness, but the powerful will be called powerfully to account; for he who is all men's master is obsequious to none, and is not overawed by greatness. Small and great alike are of his making, and all are under his providence equally, but it is the powerful for whom he reserves the sternest inquisition. To you then who have absolute power I speak, in hope that you may learn wisdom and not go astray; those who in holiness have kept a holy course, will be accounted holy, and those who have learnt that lesson will be able to make their defence. Be eager then to hear me, and long for my teaching; so you will learn (6:1-11, NEB).

From this passage, it is clear that rulers have a special responsibility to do right because of their power and privilege. They will be judged strictly on their exercise of power for the benefit of those who need justice. As a result, *oppression can never be justified in the name of the state.* Indeed, it is a travesty to invoke the Bible in support of state oppression. It teaches just the opposite—the state is for good and for justice. Less then this leads to judgment.

Since the New Testament teachings on the state are not contrary to what we have found in Hebrew Scriptures, we can say in short that *the state does not have any divine mandate or legitimation in the Bible apart from the doing of justice which is to reflect the justice of the divine sovereign.* The state reflects God's justice by implementing laws which liberate and bring substantive justice to the powerless and oppressed. This justice, by making things all right prepares the ground for the experience of shalom. This, it seems to me, is the clear teaching of both the Hebrew Scriptures and the Greek Scriptures.

Implications for shalom making

Given the biblical emphasis on the duty of the state to implement substantive justice which leads to shalom, it would seem to follow that states which deny substantive justice to the poor and oppressed must be opposed. This does not mean that there should not be procedural justice—obviously there should be and the Bible commands it. But procedural justice is only a means to an end—the law is to be liberating and promoting of shalom justice. The law is not an end in itself.

In this light, it seems that shalom makers should be more concerned with justice than with legality. If this is the case, should not *shalom makers oppose the forms of justice which maintain an unjust status quo and struggle for the realization of shalom justice in a society?* Should not Christian people unite in their opposition to laws which promote inequality and oppression?

If this makes sense in light of what we have seen, why is the church not more ready to condone and support civil disobedience as a way of resisting justice which is not substantive nor shalom producing? *Can we go further and ask whether we are for shalom if we are not opposing and even disobeying laws and a legal system from which we profit but which does not bring shalom justice to the poor and oppressed?* Is the act of obeying an unjust law from the standpoint of shalom justice an act against shalom?

8. *The prophets, the state, and shalom*

I n view of the impact which the monarchy had on Israelite society, we looked to see what ideas the people might have had about the state: what was its proper function. We found that the king was held responsible for the practice of a kind of justice which would bring shalom. This substantive justice was brought about by liberating the poor and oppressed and crushing the power of those who oppressed them (Ps. 72). This lofty vision of the role of the state led us to ask how citizens are to respond to laws and policies of governments which do not promote justice as measured by the litmus test of the oppressed and marginalized

Now we want to follow up our study of the forces at work within the biblical faith with a look at the Israelite state through the eyes of the prophets. Did the state come to fulfill the hopes of the people? Was it a liberating force for them? Did it maintain liberation? Or did Samuel's somber warning come true? As we saw in the last chapter, this latter possibility was beginning to appear under David and Solomon. In this context, how did the prophets respond? What was their message for the state and for their fellow citizens?

The prophetic critique of the state

As we read through the prophets, we find that kings were not always agents of shalom justice. The warning of Samuel came true. This is most visible in the message of the preexilic prophets, those who lived before the fall of Judah and Jerusalem and the exile to Babylonia in 587 B.C.E. Here we shall focus on the writings of the prophets who emerged in the eighth century, the 700s B.C.E., following the prophetic duo, Elijah and Elisha, who were active in the preceding century.

Amos was the first of these prophets. In reading the Book of Amos we find the message to be largely negative—accusations of present wrongdoing and predictions of coming judgment in the form of a national disaster. But if we look more closely at the message, we can see in it also a positive call, a call for justice. This call is issued, on the one hand, by denouncing those who have worked against justice:

> O [woe] to you who turn justice to wormwood, and cast down
> righteousness to the earth! (5:7).

> But you have turned justice into poison and the fruit of righ-
> teousness into wormwood (6:12).

On the other hand, he states a positive challenge: "But let justice roll
down like waters and righteousness like an everflowing stream" (5:24).
Significantly, justice and righteousness, central to the work of the state,
as we saw in the last chapter, form a goal to which Amos is calling the
elite.

Amos's message is directed largely to the leaders, probably because
they have the power to implement justice. Indeed, since they are the
ones responsible for exploiting the poor and are profiting from the lack
of justice, a large part of the book is made up of specific accusations
which point to their violations of justice.

What injustices are they guilty of? Amos focuses on how the weak
and needy are being treated. For example, in 2:6-8, he gives examples of
oppressive practices against the powerless which illustrate the lack of
shalom justice. Likewise, in 8:4-6 and 5:11, Amos critiques the lavish
lifestyle which results from such practices. See 6:1-7 where he addresses the leaders of the nation in the capital of Samaria or 4:1-3 where
he addresses their wives. Their lack of concern with shalom justice
leads to the concentration of wealth which Amos characterizes as the
storing of violence and destruction in Samaria (3:9-10). That is, the
prosperity of the capital and its elite is the result of violence and
oppression against the underclass. Since in the presence of oppression
there can be no shalom, the results of such practices—even prosperity—can never be shalom, but only judgment and destruction.

As a result, Amos saw the day of Yahweh not as a day of vindication
for Israel, which is what the people expected, but as exactly the opposite: a day of ruin and of judgment.

> Woe to you who desire the day of Yahweh!
>   Why would you have the day of Yahweh?
> It is darkness, and not light;
>   as if a man fled from a lion,
>   and a bear met him;
> or went into the house and leaned with his hand against the
> wall,
>   and a serpent bit him.
> Is not the day of Yahweh darkness, and not light,
>   and gloom with no brightness in it? (5:18-20).

Those who do not practice justice but instead oppress should not look forward to meeting God. God, the God of justice (remember Ps. 82), will bring judgment upon oppressors. The message of Amos seems clear—practice real justice, a substantive justice which makes for shalom, instead of taking advantage by reason of power and position.

It is significant that the critique of Amos is not based on the letter of the law—procedural correctness or legality—but on the spirit and aim of the law—liberation and shalom.[1] For example, Amos condemns those who sell others into slavery, apparently because of debts (2:6). Now the law allowed for people to be sold into debt slavery. (See Exod. 21:1ff, for example.) But here the issue for Amos appears to be whether such a practice promotes justice when those being sold are at an economic disadvantage and, in fact, are being victimized even in the buying of food (Amos 8:4-6). Amos's answer is clear, regardless of what laws may or may not apply—the procedural question—the outcome must be justice—a substantive justice which brings about rightness between people instead of the treasures of violence.

Amos was not alone in the call for justice and righteousness (all rightness). Isaiah too is concerned with justice.

> learn to do good;
> seek justice,
>   correct oppression;
> defend the fatherless,
>   plead for the widow (1:17).

> For the vineyard of Yahweh of hosts
>   is the house of Israel,
> and the men of Judah
>   are [God's] pleasant planting;
> and [God] looked for justice,   .
>   but behold, bloodshed;
> for righteousness,
>   but behold, a cry [from the oppressed]! (5:7).

The expectation of God was that shalom justice would be realized among the covenant people. But when they were examined, instead of justice, violence and oppression were found. As in Amos, the lack of justice was measured by the treatment of the poor and weak: if these—

---

1. Eryl W. Davies, *Prophecy and Ethics: Isaiah and the Ethical Tradition of Israel* (Sheffield: JSOT Press, 1981), in a study of similar material in Isaiah concludes that Isaiah's message cannot be accounted for on the basis of the laws now in the Bible. Indeed, many of the practices which Isaiah denounced may have had a legal basis in the society. The same is true of Amos.

the fatherless and widows—are not living in shalom, then oppression not justice is being promoted. As a result, the positive call of the prophet is for the people to do justice, to look out for the needs of the weak—orphans and widows—and to liberate the oppressed.

The prophets' concern with substantive justice finds perhaps its clearest expression in Isaiah when he proclaims:

> Woe to the legislators of infamous laws,
> to those who issue tyrannical decrees,
> who refuse justice to the unfortunate
> and cheat the poor among my people of their rights,
> who make widows their prey
> and rob the orphan (10:1-2 JB).

Those who control the making of laws can make them for their own advantage and to the harm of those who have no power and no voice in political decision making. As a result, it is all too easy for the law to injure the powerless and disadvantaged and benefit those with power and advantage. It is this legality which benefits the haves but which does not liberate or lead to shalom which Isaiah denounces. Rather a justice which brings about rightness must be implemented so the oppressed and powerless may be liberated and gain well-being.

General calls for the practice of justice from other prophets could be cited, such as Micah 6:8 to further illustrate how pivotal was the establishment of justice for the message of these prophets. In addition, we could refer to many specific passages where individual illustrations of social oppression are denounced. (See Isa. 1:10-17; 10:1-2; 3:13-15; Micah 3:9-12; 6:11-12; Hosea 12:7-9; Jer. 21:11-12; 7:3-7.) But we will mention just one more judgment speech, Jeremiah 22:3-5, which is addressed specifically to the king.

> Do justice and righteousness, and deliver from the hand of the oppressor him who has been robbed. And do no wrong or violence to the alien, the fatherless, and the widow, nor shed innocent blood in this place. For if you will indeed obey this word, then there shall enter the gates of this house kings who sit on the throne of David, riding in chariots and on horses, they, and their servants, and their people. But if you will not heed these words, I swear by myself, says Yahweh, that this house shall become a desolation.

The way of life and the way of death were put before the king: do shalom justice and live. The dynasty will continue. Or, continue the present state of affairs and the end will surely come. But as Jeremiah

22:13-17 illustrates, the king was only concerned with injustice and gain, luxury, and conspicuous consumption. For Jeremiah in relaying God's message, this could only mean the judgment of God will come, because God stands against all oppression and for shalom.

As we have seen from this brief survey of the message of the eighth-century prophets, they mention over and over again the disadvantaged in Israelite society: the poor, widows, orphans, and noncitizens (aliens). Since it is the duty of a state to promote justice, the most needy are the barometer from which can be read how well the rulers are fulfilling the obligations of office. As a result, the distribution of resources within the society becomes the key test of how the political system is working since the elite both profit from the present system and govern the nation as well.[2] This explains why most of the examples given by the prophets of injustice lie in the economic sphere. It is here that the proper or improper distribution of resources is most clearly seen. It is here that it is plain who were the winners and the victims of the system. The prophetic critique is then at the same time an economic one—improper distribution, and a political one—the lack of justice. It seems from this perspective that *economics and politics are inseparable.*

Military force and justice

The prophets did more than denounce oppression and call for justice. They also criticized the use of force which maintained the unjust status quo. In their critique, the prophets combined military power with idolatry. Hosea sees the day when Israel will have a change of heart, then the people will confess their iniquity and say, "Assyria shall not save us, we will not ride upon horses; and we will say no more 'Our God,' to the work of our hands. In thee the orphan finds mercy" (Hos. 14:3). In the future, he implies, the people will renounce foreign alliances, military might, and idolatry all in the same breath. Then comes the reminder that the true God, Yahweh, is a God of shalom justice who cares for those of the underclass. Here lies the true strength of the nation. (See also the stirring passages in Isa. 30:1-5, 15-16; 31:1-3.)

Likewise, in Isaiah 2:6-8 and Micah 5:9-14, horses and chariots, fortresses and other military items are mentioned in lists which include divination, idolatry, and economic oppression. In what ways are military might and idolatry related to oppression?

Force which is used to maintain the economic and political status quo cuts the nerve of shalom justice. It props up a social order which benefits the rulers and elite and provides them with little incentive to

2. For a study of the coalescence of economic, political, and military factors in Israelite society, see John A. Dearman, "Property Rights in the Eighth-century Prophets: The Conflict and Its Background," PhD. dissertation, Emory University, 1981.

improve the lot of the underclass. This policy can easily bolster the view that the destiny of the nation depends on the power of its armies rather than on justice. For the prophets, evidently, such reliance was akin to idolatry—a state atheism for which God and God's demands for justice make no practical difference in the arrangements of government. Thus, for the prophets, the judgment of God would be on both their oppression and on the military through which they held power. Or, on the other hand, since justice was the foundation of a king's rule (Jer. 22:1-5), depending on anything else was a vain hope and judgment was sure to come.

> You have plowed iniquity,
>   you have reaped injustice,
>   you have eaten the fruit of lies.
> Because you have trusted in your chariots
>   and in the multitude of your warriors,
> therefore the tumult of war shall arise among your people,
>   and all your fortresses shall be destroyed (Hos. 10:13-14).

The same connection is also made in Isaiah 30:12.

From this point of view, we can see a relation between the state's reliance on force and the presence of injustice. On the other hand, we would expect a link between the practice of shalom justice and the decreasing use of force. In the latter case, rather than keeping the underclass down by force and power, their needs are met. Justice becomes the key to political power, not domination. We can illustrate this as follows:

+ violence	- violence
- justice	+ justice

The prophets found, then, that shalom could not exist where the state depended on force to rule and maintain itself and ignored justice. Strength does not bring shalom, but justice does. And where justice is denied, judgment will follow since oppression stands under the judgment of the God who wills shalom. Military strength in the long run could not preserve a nation that would not practice justice.

Shalom versus shalom

Now not all the prophets in ancient Israel agreed that injustice, violence, and the lack of health in the society would in the end bring the fall of the state and the destruction of the nation. Some thought things would turn out all right and shalom would come. Often, the majority would agree that things would be okay, while a minority, sometimes only a single prophet, would see things differently, prophesying doom and gloom instead of shalom. We can see this difference in outlook from the charges Jeremiah brought against the shalom prophets, the false prophets.

> For from the least to the greatest of them,
>   every one is greedy for unjust gain;
> and from prophet to priest,
>   every one deals falsely.
> They have healed the wound of my people lightly,
>   saying "Peace, peace,"
> when there is no peace (6:13-14).

> Yahweh said to me, "Do not pray for the welfare of this people. Though they fast, I will not hear their cry, and though they offer burnt offering and cereal offering, I will not accept them; but I will consume them by the sword, by famine, and by pestilence." Then I said: "Ah, Lord Yahweh, behold, the prophets say to them, 'You shall not see the sword, nor shall you have famine, but I will give you assured peace in this place.' " And Yahweh said to me: "The prophets are prophesying lies in my name; I did not send them, nor did I command them or speak to them. They are prophesying to you a lying vision, worthless divination, and the deceit of their own minds" (14:11-14). [See also Jeremiah 23:7; 27:9, 14; 28:8.]

The false prophets, involved in the unjust social order of the day, seemed able to harmonize shalom with the presence of social injustice. Shalom perhaps seemed more a matter of national security than national justice. For Jeremiah, destruction not shalom followed injustice. Shalom simply was not at home with the oppressions of the present regime. Either people would change and work for justice or the nation would be destroyed. (Remember Jeremiah's message to the king quoted above.) Either way, a change was coming since the poor living in poverty and oppression alongside the wealthy with more than they needed was an unjust situation. This state of affairs could not be patched up by saying shalom, shalom, and trusting in the nation's military and foreign alliances to preserve the nation.

Ezekiel repeats this point of view by scolding the false prophets who merely whitewash matters by saying shalom, shalom (Ezek. 13). Where substantive social justice is not being practiced, there can be no shalom. (See chapter 2 for a fuller discussion of the meaning of shalom as it relates to the debate between true and false prophets.)

Clearly, for the prophets of shalom caught profiting from the oppression of the underclass, shalom came to mean the well-being of the state and those who profit from its operation rather than the well-being of the nation as a whole including the underclasses. State shalom which thrives on oppression has replaced God's shalom rooted in liberation and substantive justice for the poor and oppressed. Against such states the true prophets declared the judgment of God. *In this context, religion which supports such state shalom stands in opposition to God's shalom. Rather than being an agency of justice and well-being it is false religion*—it is not from God (Jer. 23:9-40).

It should be clear from this interprophetic dispute that religion is not necessarily liberating. As the false prophets illustrate, since religious leaders and institutions also profit, indeed may become quite wealthy, they may lend their voices in support of oppressors and against those working for justice and shalom. They may often stand with the haves and the powerful rather than with the have-nots and the powerless. As a result, *religion has often been a conservative force supporting the well-to-do, the haves, at the expense of the weak and have-nots. Shalom makers must oppose this perversion of biblical religion*.

The state revisited

What went wrong? As we saw in the last chapter, the state was supposed to be an instrument for shalom justice. It was to govern the people by putting an end to chaos, corruption, and injustice. It was to provide security. Instead, it became an instrument for injustice, or, at least, it did not act to promote justice. It relied on the use of force to maintain order rather than promoting the proper order of justice. As a result, rather than promoting security, it brought on insecurity both internally and externally. Why were the people's hopes for the state not realized? Why did the state not fulfill its own ideal foundation which was based on the doing of substantive social justice thereby promoting shalom in the land?

The answer to these questions has two parts: first, we need to understand the economic shift which took place in the country as a result of the increasing social complexity and the rise of the state as discussed in the last chapter. Then, we need to look at the relationship of the state to this economic shift.

The new economics

With the rise of the monarchy and immediately following, a new economic system and mentality emerged which worked against social justice. The reasons for the rise of new economic practices seem to be rooted in the changes brought by the monarchy as outlined in the last chapter—the rise of prebendal estates in which land was a resource to be exploited for the sake of an urban elite, the need to collect taxes to support the state which concentrated resources in the capital and probably other urban centers, and the concentration of power (political, economic, and military) into a few hands, without checks and balances, and to the detriment of taditional forms of government and economic practice.[3]

In this context, the kings should have implemented liberating laws and shalom justice. What this would have looked like can be seen most clearly from what we have called the reform texts. (See our discussion above on these laws.) These texts are based on the following convictions: the land and other resources are God's; people are just stewards of them; resources are to be used to meet community need, as in Deuteronomy 15:9-11, and title to the resource cannot be changed, as in Leviticus 25:14-17, 25-28. Since the present user is a steward, the resources are open to use by others in the community, the gleaning laws being an example. They are not for the exclusive use of the owner and their product is not for the owner's own consumption alone. Distribution was to be from those who had to those who were in need.

However, as people came to regard themselves as owners, they came to view the land or other capital as their own and its product as their exclusive right. In the case of the holders of prebendal estates, it was the king who gave it to them, so title could be transferred. It was given for their use, to support them in their urban setting. They wanted to exchange this product for gain because they were interested in obtaining luxury items, items of prestige. (See the comments of Amos in 3:14-15 and 6:1-6.)

The gap between the poor and wealthy became greater; poverty and affluence existing side by side in the society came to be expected. It seemed normal because now the underclass had no way out as they came to be deprived of the very economic factors, like land, to which previously they had had an inalienable right. Deprived of land, forced to buy food in the market, they indeed did become slaves with no place to go (Amos 2:6; 8:4-6).

The meaning of this development can be seen more clearly when we contast in outline form the basic values and premises of the economics of shalom found in the laws with the economics of wealth practiced by the elite. The following outline is based on the reform legislation and a

---

3. On the concentration of resources and the inability of the Israelite political system to provide checks and balances, so that the legal and executive system became tools of the elite for concentration of wealth rather than an instrument of substantive justice, see the works of Dearman and Davies cited above. Also Bernhard Lang, "The Social Organization of Peasant Poverty in Biblical Israel," JSOT 24(1982)47-63.

few other laws to sketch the economics of shalom position, while the economics of wealth is determined largely from the negative criticisms of the prophets.

The principles of the economics of shalom and economics of wealth

	Economics of Shalom	Wealth Economics
1. Ownership of subsistence resources	God owns, people use Lev. 25:14-17, 25-28, 29-31; Deut. 15:7-8	People own; exclude rights of others Isa. 5:8
2. Access to resources	Open; gleaning, sabbatical laws Exod. 23:10-11; Deut. 15:7-11	Closed, exclusive rights to owner; concentration of resources Isa. 5:8
3. Consumption	Based on need; wants balanced by surplus Deut. 14:28-29; 15:1-11	Based on self-aggrandizement Amos 6:1-6; 3:15
4. Distribution mechanism	Unbalanced reciprocity; based on need—from the haves to the have-nots 2 Cor. 8:14; Luke 6:27-36	Exchange for gain, based on getting more than giving; flow from have-nots to haves Amos 8:4ff; 2:6-8
5. Basic outlook	There is enough; trust and reliance on God 2 Cor. 9:8, 10-11	Scarcity, so hoard; security is in saving for the future Amos 3:10
6. Basic value	Affluence is measured by leisure over against work for subsistence	Affluence is based on having more than others Amos 6:1-6
7. Disposition of surplus	To those in need 2 Cor. 8.14; Deut. 14:28-29, 15:1-11	Accumulate to support separate classes Amos 4:1; 6:1-6
8. Goal	Finite; the subsistence of all Deut. 15:1-11	Infinite; wealth, people never have enough Amos 8:5-6

9. Results	a. Stewardship of resources b. Justice, no needy or oppressed Deut. 15:4; Acts 4:32-34; 11:27-30; 2:43-46 c. Minimal force needed to maintain the system	a. Exploitation of resources b. Class separation; wealth in the midst of poverty c. Oppression and increasing force to maintain class separation

Why did kings not intervene to reform the situation when social justice was no longer being done? Why didn't the state act to implement shalom justice? To answer this question we will take a brief look at some ideas which are suggested by anthropologists from their study of present societies about the nature of states and how they arise.

The development of the state

States arise, according to one view, when the unit of production is no longer the unit of consumption. We saw this shift occurring between the period of the judges and of the kings in the previous chapter. In this case, a society tends to divide into two classes: those who are called upon to produce a surplus and those who have need of the surplus. The state steps in to regulate relationships between these two classes. Thus a state seems to arise to solve internal tensions as society becomes more complex and diverse. In theory, the state should aid all persons in the society by maintaining equality between the various groups.[4]

The state has the power to regulate relationships within a society, because "a true state . . . is distinguishable . . . by the presence of that special form of control, the consistent threat of force by a body of persons legitimately constituted to use it. Personal force, as in feuding may be found at all levels, but in states it is the monopoly of only certain persons."[5] This force can be used to maintain and promote justice. The responsibility to regulate class relationships, however, can become narrowly defined as maintaining order. This perception becomes a stumbling block to the state becoming an instrument for real justice since as Fried writes, "At the heart of the problem of maintaining the general order is the need to defend the central order of stratification—the differentiation of categories of population in terms of access to basic

4. Lawrence Krader, "The Origin of the State Among the Nomads of Asia," in *Pastoral Production and Society* (Cambridge: Cambridge University Press, 1979), pp. 221ff.

5. Elmer Service, *Primitive Social Organization: An Evolutionary Perspective* (New York: Random House, 1962), p. 171.

resources."[6] As a result, the state is constantly tempted (or compelled?) because of its commitment to maintaining order, to define justice as procedural justice which maintains an order of unequal access to life resources. Often, or even usually, the state then ends up defending, in the name of justice, a status quo which operates for the benefit of some against the well-being of others in the society.

This seems to be what happened in Israel. Using an illustration from the last chapter, in 1 Samuel 25:1-11, we have the story of a confrontation between Nabal, a rich herder who belonged to the elite, and men from David's band made up of those who were economically dispossessed (1 Sam. 22:2-5). We clearly see in this meeting representatives of two economic classes: Nabal, representing those who control great resources and, as a result, are able to live in luxury; and David's men, who are fugitives for economic reasons. They were asking a gift from Nabal since while his flocks were in their region they left them alone. Nabal does not want to pay. This for two reasons: first, because many servants are rebelling against their lords—there seems to be widespread dissatisfaction by serfs against their masters. Second, he gets his income from sources which he owns and works; why should he give up some of his product to those whom he doesn't know and who haven't worked (economics of wealth)? Clearly, this struggle between the haves and the have-nots needed a solution. This was one of the hopes for the state; it would promote internal justice (1 Sam. 8:1-3).

The state, however, when it arose in Israel, rather than addressing this problem and acting for social justice by opening up access to resources became itself part of the elite and operated for their own interests. The king and the officers at court seem to have become major landholders. What benefited the elite benefited them. In this situation, they had little incentive to slow down the flow of resources into the hands of a few and the increase of individual wealth at the cost of poverty for many.

This development was bound to bring a reaction. Two types of response are typical to this development. One is labeled reactive: here the attempt is to return to a simpler era, the era before the state. In Israel, this move may have been represented by the Rechabites, whose lifestyle represents that of a bygone era. (See Jer. 35.) This would also represent the position of some antikingship sentiments in the Bible, as for example in 1 Samuel 8 where kingship is equated with apostasy. True faith is only possible, in this view, in the absence of kingship.[7]

6. Morton H. Fried, *The Evolution of Political Society: An Essay in Political Anthropology* (New York: Random House, 1967), p. 229.

7. For a discussion of the variety of pro and con kingship arguments in the Bible, see Frank Crusemann, *Der Widerstand gegen das Königtum: Die antiköniglichen Texte des Alten Testamentes und der Kampf um den frühen israelitischen Staat* (Wissenschaftliche Monographien. Neukirchen-Vluyn: Neukirchener Verlag, 1978).

On the other hand, others go along with the state: they want to reform the state rather than reject it altogether. They see the state as valuable, but want to divide up the pie differently.[8] This seems to represent the position of the prophets. They were against the unjust practices of reigning kings, but were not against kingship per se. Jeremiah 22:1-5 is a good example of this concern. Jeremiah places before the king the option—choose to do justice and kings will continue to reign in Israel. Or, choose to continue doing injustice and the dynasty will come to an end. Here there is no opposition to the institution of kingship, but rather to the way it is exercised. The critical key is shalom justice—if the state uses its power to implement and maintain equity and aid for the powerless and poor then the state is operating okay, and there can be shalom. However, if the state operates mainly according to procedural justice and uses its power to maintain the separation between the rich and the poor, then the state must be reshaped so that it can operate as it should.

The state and shalom

From our brief, in fact, skimpy, historical survey of the development of kingship in Israel as seen against the background of modern work in anthropology, we can understand that the state is not in theory against shalom but it can easily become co-opted into maintaining law and order justice which promotes and protects the haves against the have-nots. This maintenance of social injustice, we have argued, leads to the state needing to adopt an increasing capacity for violence and force in order to maintain itself and the central order of stratification. This use of force to maintain inequity can of course be done at any level, internally as well as externally on the international scene.

Since this state of affairs is the exact opposite of shalom, *shalom makers must oppose all states who protect and maintain such stratification and concentration of resources*. In this opposition, the shalom maker favors neither anarchism nor a return to a pre-state society; but like the prophets, the peacemaker is for a political and economic system which works for shalom and against oppression.

I hope it is clear by now, that the issue of shalom justice and economics is a structural one which cannot be solved on the individual level. The state is that form of social structure and organization which must meet these needs. Therefore, *one goal of the shalom maker is to transform the political system and the people who operate it so that a state will arise which does aim at shalom justice*. To what extent this

---

8. Richard N. Adams, "Rural Collective Action and the State: A Discussion," in *Forging Nations: A Comparative View of Rural Ferment and Revolt*, eds., J. Spielberg and S. Whiteford (East Lansing: Michigan State University Press, 1976), pp. 150-67.

can happen in any situation is an open question. *What does seem clear is that unless we move toward the realization of substantive social justice within the society, we will not be able to move toward shalom.* ⟵ More than this, it also seems clear that as long as we are willing to sit and watch the practice of injustice, especially if we benefit from it, we can hardly say that we are for shalom. *Shalom makers must be involved in changing the politics of oppression into the politics of liberation and shalom.*

The messianic hope

It is against this background of the prophets' critique of the present state that we can understand their vision of the future. While they kept reminding the ruling elite of their duty to provide justice, measured by how well the weakest elements of the society were having their needs met, we know that their appeal went unheeded.

In the short run, then, the prophets prophesied that doom would come upon the nation since God's judgment was squarely upon those who stood in the way of shalom justice. In the long run, however, the prophets hoped for a different future for God's people.

When the prophets looked to the future, they entertained the hope that some day a king would arise who would implement God's will for justice. In these passages, they express the vision of a new king who will do as kings should do. In other words, their vision projected into the future their present understanding of the proper function of the state; present critique was the basis for the future hope.[9]

In this connection, we should note what has often been pointed out. The prophets called for no peasants' revolt, no new system of government. For them, the system was not the issue, but justice. If a government supported shalom justice so that the underclasses were helped, then the government was on the right road.[10] If it did not, then it stood condemned. The issue was how the system operated—the results— not the type of system itself. But it should be clearly understood, *the prophets' critique and the coming destruction of the state, coupled with their vision of the future when the state would operate as it should, implies that states which operate and promote injustice must be transformed into justly working ones or be destroyed.*

9. On the future vision of the prophets as a continuation of present royal ideology see Moshe Weinfeld, "Zion and Jerusalem as Religious and Political Capital: Ideology and Utopia," in *The Poet and the Historian: Essays in Literary and Historical Biblical Criticism*, ed., Richard E. Friedman (Chico, Calif.: Scholars Press: 1983), pp. 75-115.

10. Two remarks may be in order here. First, a king who did justice might be such a different king that, in fact, he would represent a different type of government. Second, since we today do have various options in the economic and political realm, we should choose those which are most conducive to shalom justice.

This vision of the future is often called the messianic vision or hope. In Hebrew Scriptures, the word *meshiach*, which is our English word *messiah*, refers to one who is anointed. Usually it is used of the king of Israel or Judah, like David or Saul, because part of the protocol in becoming king was to be anointed. In a few places, *messiah* is also used of the high priest (Lev. 4:3, 5, 16), presumably because he also was anointed as part of the ritual in coming to office. Because the king was the anointed one, and because these visionary passages talk about a future royal figure, these passages are called messianic.

The series of messianic passages begins with the preexilic prophets, especially Isaiah, continues with the exilic prophets, and on into the postexilic prophets. We will cite several examples from these prophecies to indicate their flavor:

> Give counsel,
>   grant justice;
> make your shade like night
>   at the height of noon;
> hide the outcasts,
>   betray not the fugitive;
> let the outcasts of Moab
>   sojourn among you;
> be a refuge to them
>   from the destroyer.
> When the oppressor is no more,
>   and destruction has ceased,
> and he who tramples under foot
>   has vanished from the land,
> then a throne will be established in steadfast love
>   and on it will sit in faithfulness
>   in the tent of David
> one who judges and seeks justice
>   and is swift to do righteousness (Isa. 16:3-5).

Behold, the days are coming, says Yahweh when I will raise up for David a righteous Branch, and he shall reign as king and deal wisely, and shall execute justice and righteousness in the land. In his days Judah will be saved, and Israel will dwell securely. And this is the name by which he will be called: "Yahweh is our righteousness" (Jer. 23:5-6).

> Rejoice greatly, O daughter of Zion!
>   Shout aloud, O daughter of Jerusalem!
> Lo, your king comes to you;
>   triumphant and victorious is he,

humble and riding on an ass,
   on a colt the foal of an ass.
I will cut off the chariot from Ephraim
   and the war horse from Jerusalem;
and the battle bow shall be cut off,
   and he shall command peace to the nations;
his dominion shall be from sea to sea,
   and from the River to the ends of the earth (Zech. 9:9-10).

In these words, it is easy to see the continuity with the prophets' critique. Note especially the theme of justice and rightness. This theme is especially stressed by the preexilic prophets who, as we have seen, emphasized justice and righteousness in their confrontation with the people and the state. There is also the note of peace being brought about by the kings' just reign. (See also Isa. 9:1-6; 11:1-9; 32:1ff, 15-17; Micah 5:2-4a; Jer. 33:14-18.)

In the exilic and postexilic prophecies, following the destruction of Jerusalem and the temple which was understood as God's judgment, the emphasis tends to be more on peace as in the Zechariah passage. This peace is brought about first of all by God as an act of deliverance of Israel from the nations round about it. (See also Ezek. 34:23-24; 37:22, 24-25; Hag. 2:21-23; Zech. 6:9-14.)

Besides these passages in which a royal figure is mentioned, we also have two other types of passages which relate the prophets' expectation for the future.

It shall come to pass in the latter days
   that the mountain of the house of Yahweh
shall be established as the highest of the mountains,
   and shall be raised above the hills;
and all the nations shall flow to it,
   and many peoples shall come, and say:
"Come, let us go up to the mountain of Yahweh,
   to the house of the God of Jacob;
that he may teach us his ways
   and that we may walk in his paths."
For out of Zion shall go forth the law,
   and the word of Yahweh from Jerusalem.
He shall judge between the nations,
   and shall decide for many peoples;
and they shall beat their swords into plowshares,
   and their spears into pruning hooks;
nation shall not lift up sword against nation,
   neither shall they learn war any more (Isa. 2:2-4; Micah 4.1-3).

Since we have already quoted this passage in chapter 2 we shall only note here briefly how it ties in with the prophets' general messianic expectations. Here there is no mention of a king as an intermediary; instead the emphasis is on God and God's sovereignty which is manifested from the holy city and temple. This too is connected with royal ideology, as the capital city is not only the place of the king's throne but of God's as well. Although the imagery is thus shifted, the emphasis is still the same: when God's future comes, justice and peace will be done.[11]

A second type of passage in which a hope for the future is seen expressed is found in a series of poems in Isaiah 40-55 which center around a servant figure who will do God's will. The poem which most clearly and forcefully expresses the theme of justice is Isaiah 42:1-4:

> Behold my servant, whom I uphold,
>   my chosen, in whom my soul delights;
> I have put my Spirit upon him,
>   he will bring forth justice to the nations.
> He will not cry or lift up his voice,
>   or make it heard in the street;
> a bruised reed he will not break,
>   and a dimly burning wick he will not quench;
>   he will faithfully bring forth justice.
> He will not fail or be discouraged
>   till he has established justice in the earth;
>   and the coastlands wait for his law.

Although the figure is here called a servant, yet the future hope is similar; through justice, God's will is to be realized. The exact meaning of justice in this passage has been much debated. It would seem that it has something to do with Israel's fate as a people conquered and in captivity and with the role of Cyrus as their liberator and restorer. In this context, the Hebrew word *mishpat* seems not so much to have the forensic sense of case or procedural justice, but more the sense of decision made on behalf of someone, here a decision made for substantive justice toward Israel. God has a plan to liberate Israel and restore it. The servant announces this plan, and thereby serves notice to all that the God of Israel is God alone, because only Israel's God can act to

---

11. See Weinfeld, "Zion and Jerusalem," for the interrelatedness of royal and divine glory in the capital city. According to him, since these two motifs are conjoined in the Ancient Near East, they should not be taken as separate visions of the future—e.g., one with a king and one without a king, but God ruling directly. Thus the omission of a royal figure in the passage just quoted is not necessarily evidence of a nonroyal future vision.

liberate a powerless people from their conqueror. This is the justice of the servant.

In the next chapter, we shall go on to study the ministry and teachings of Jesus in light of the expectation by the prophets that one day there would be a figure who would rule justly for the poor and oppressed and through whose rule God's will would be realized and shalom experienced among people.

What seems significant about the prophets' vision for us is that peacemakers live in the conviction that God does will shalom. One way in which this shalom is realized is through the practice of justice by the state. Indeed, as we have just seen, just as justice was basic for God's rule, so also justice is the foundation of the state. But we have also seen that states easily side with the the powerful against the powerless, the haves against the have-nots. In this context, the shalom maker struggles by resisting laws which are unjust and by working toward the practice of real shalom justice.

Even though in the present, in spite of our struggles, justice is not always realized, we should not give up hope, but live in the light of a longer view of history—liberation and justice will not be denied; they are in the plan of God. God's decision, the servant announces, is for justice. *Thus in spite of weakness—like Israel in exile—shalom makers struggle to transform the present reality by pointing to a picture of what history should be like.*

9. Jesus: the messiah of God

T he prophet's hope for a future in which God's justice and shalom would be realized on earth was alive in the New Testament period. We can see this expectation shining through in the early chapters of the Gospel of Luke, particularly in its hymns.

For instance, in the announcement of Jesus' birth to Mary, an angel says he will be given the throne of David, reign over Israel, and his kingdom shall have no end: a clear witness to the hope for a royal messianic figure. This king's reign will be marked by shalom justice, just as the prophets envisioned.

> And his mercy is on those who fear him
> from generation to generation.
> He has shown strength with his arm,
> he has scattered the proud in the imagination of their hearts,
> he has put down the mighty from their thrones,
> and exalted those of low degree;
> he has filled the hungry with good things,
> and the rich he has sent empty away (Luke 1:50-53).

With aid for the needy and powerless comes the wish that Israel will be freed from its enemies. Following this liberation / salvation, the messiah will bring about faithfulness and obedience to God. (See Luke 1:68-79; 2:29-32.)

A second pointer to expectations for the coming messiah centers around John the Baptist. In Luke 3:10-14, 18, when people ask what they should do to escape God's judgment, they are told to act justly.

> And the multitudes asked him, "What then shall we do?" And he answered them, "He who has two coats, let him share with him who has none; and he who has food, let him do likewise." Tax collectors also came to be baptized, and said to him, "Teacher, what shall we do?" And he said to them, "Collect no more than is appointed to you." Soldiers also asked him, "And we, what

shall we do?" And he said to them, "Rob no one by violence or by false accusation, and be content with your wages." . . . So with many other exhortations, he preached good news to the people.

The good news of John was the good news of shalom justice. Those who had goods were to help those who had needs. Others were admonished to exercise their offices justly, rather than for their own enrichment.

Because of this message, the people were wondering whether or not he was the messiah. Evidently, in this proclamation of the good news of shalom justice, he triggered the people's expectations.

Jesus the messiah

As we saw in the chapter on the atonement, the basic affirmation made in Greek Scriptures about Jesus is that he was the Christ. Now we have become so used to the phrase *Jesus Christ*, that we take Christ as a proper name; it is Jesus' last name. So if Jesus filled out a form calling for last name first, he would write: Christ, Jesus! In fact, however, originally *Christ* was not a name, but a title. It is the Greek translation of the Hebrew word *meshiach*, messiah.

But to what extent can we say that Jesus really was the messiah? Is the claim that Jesus was the messiah based purely on faith, or does hard evidence support this claim? In the chapter on the atonement, we suggested that this title, in fact, goes back to Jesus himself.

So, to rephrase this question: What about his life and teachings would make this claim credible? What were his messianic credentials? In the following section, we will use the picture of Jesus given us in the Gospel of Luke to demonstrate what evidence might ground this claim. In the end, we wish to suggest that his teaching and actions as presented here can be understood within the framework of this claim.[1]

In Luke 4:16-30, we find what we may call Jesus' inaugural address. In the other Synoptic Gospels, this event occurs later in Jesus' ministry. (See Matt. 13:53-58; Mark 6:1-6.) Luke, however, places it at the beginning of Jesus' public ministry, evidently because it contains for Luke a basic statement of Jesus' purpose. In this version, Jesus reads from the prophet Isaiah:

---

1. I have been especially helped in my reading of Luke by the following sources: Robert B. Sloan Jr., *The Favorable Year of the Lord: A Study of Jubilary Theology in the Gospel of Luke* (Austin, Texas: Schola Press, 1977); Thomas Hoyt Jr., *The Poor in Luke-Acts*, Ph.D. dissertation, Duke University, 1974; James A. Sanders, "Second Isaiah 61 to Luke 4," in *Christianity, Judaism and Other Greco-Roman Cults: Studies for Morton Smith at Sixty*, ed. Jacob Neusner (Leiden: Brill, 1975), pp. 75-106; John Howard Yoder, *The Politics of Jesus* (Grand Rapids, Michigan: William B. Eerdmans Publ. Co., 1972); Helen R. Graham, *There Shall Be No Poor Among You: Essays in Lukan Theology* (Quezon City, Philippines: JMC Press, 1978).

The Spirit of Yahweh is upon me,
because [God] has anointed me to preach good news to the
poor.
[God] has sent me to proclaim release to the captives
and recovering of sight to the blind,
to set at liberty those who are oppressed,
to proclaim the acceptable year of Yahweh (vv. 18-19).

The passage Jesus reads is Isaiah 61:1-2a. But a phrase from these verses, namely, "brokenhearted" is omitted. In its place are words from Isaiah 58:6, "sets at liberty the oppressed." By this substitution, it seems, emphasis is being given to the physical, material aspect of Jesus' ministry. That is, we might want to spiritualize or psychologize his ministry by reading the brokenhearted as referring to those in spiritual need. And we might be tempted to spiritualize also the poor into the spiritual poor. But this substitution of "sets at liberty the oppressed" for "brokenhearted" seems to show that we must take this Scripture at face value. It refers to material, physical problems from which Jesus will liberate people. At the beginning of his ministry, Jesus announces, according to Luke, that he will be meeting the physical needs of the needy, he will be doing God's work of liberation and shalom justice.[2]

While this task is clearly on the agenda of the Messiah as we saw in the last chapter, Isaiah 61:1-2 is not a messianic passage. That is, it is not about a royal ruler. But it seems clear that the goals set forth are the deeds of the messiah, they are about shalom justice.

Luke presents further evidence that shalom justice and liberation point to Jesus as the messiah. In Luke 7:18-23, John is in prison and is having doubts about whether Jesus is the messiah. He sends two of his disciples to Jesus to ask him point-blank if he is the one who is coming or whether they are to wait for another. Jesus answers by pointing to what he is doing; Jesus heals the blind, lame, lepers, deaf; the dead are raised; and "the poor have good news preached to them." These physical signs of liberation are offered as proof to John that he is indeed the messiah. Here Jesus' messiahship is based on his acts of liberation for those in need of healing, life, and escape from poverty.[3]

But this is not all. Jesus concludes these proofs of his messiahship by saying, "And blessed is he who takes no offense at me." Why would anyone take offense at the healing of people, or even the raising of them

2. Among scholars there is a long and heated debate about what goes back to Jesus and what does not. Here when 'Jesus' is used, you may read, 'Jesus is presented as . . .' I have chosen, in this popular format, to forego this and similar locutions.

3. Note how close the list of those aided in Luke 4:16-19 and 7:18-23 match the list in Psalm 146.

from the dead? For example, this episode is preceded by Jesus raising to life the son of the widow at Nain—who would not rejoice at this turn of affairs? The answer would seem to be no one. As a result, Jesus' warning about taking offense at him probably refers particularly to the last type of evidence which he cited—the poor are receiving good news!

When we think of Jesus' ministry as presented in the Gospels, we are well aware of his healing activity; this is common. But that Jesus was good news for the materially poor is not so clear to us. What can be offered in order to support this claim? Furthermore, it is not clear in what sense this would be a stumbling block to people—why would Jesus give a warning about the offensiveness of this aspect of his ministry?

To answer these questions, let us look at how the ministry of Jesus is presented in the stories which are found only in Luke, since this material emphasizes Jesus as good news for the needy. This emphasis is not limited to this material—we are just limiting ourselves in this way to keep the length of our presentation manageable![4]

Let's begin with Luke 6:20-26, which contains the Beatitudes. However, in Luke they are different than in Matthew 5, the version with which we are most familiar. In Luke, they are in second person direct address. "Blessed are *you*. . . ." Also, they are physical and material in nature: instead of *poor in spirit*, we find just *poor*. Furthermore, they are paralleled by something new: a series of woes. Woe to the rich, the well fed, for they will receive their judgment. Already from this brief passage we can see that if you were a poor person listening to Jesus teach that poor people have the kingdom, but the wealthy will have woe, this would have been interesting. If you were well-off, this may well have been offensive.

gives examples

The teaching of the Beatitudes—blessed are the poor, woe to the rich—is illustrated by the parable in 16:19-31, the story of the rich man and Lazarus. Here the rich man had his pleasures in this life, but ended up in Hades in the next. Lazarus, the poor man, suffered in this life, but ended up in the bosom of Abraham in the next. The poor would probably have responded to such a story by saying this is good news; the rich by scratching their heads and saying there must be something wrong with this man's theology.

Or again, in chapter 18:18-22, we find the story of the rich young ruler who wanted to have eternal life; we might say, be saved. Jesus tells

4. For example, we could cite the teachings of Jesus about the kingdom of God. These teachings, of course, lie at the very heart of his ministry and mission. What we would find there is essentially identical with what we find in Luke's special material. See Carlos Abesamis, *Where Are We Going: Heaven or New World?* (Foundation Books: Manila, 1983). For a perspective from the Gospel of Mark, see his *On Mark and the New World* (Manila: Socio Pastoral Institute, 1983).

him to sell what he has and distribute it to the poor. Great news for the poor! But for the rich young ruler, the news is not so good; Jesus is a stumbling block. He goes away sad. But in the next chapter, in 19:1-10, the opposite happens. Jesus has dinner with Zacchaeus, a rich tax collector. During the course of the meal, Jesus' message evidently hits home. Thereupon, Zacchaeus announces that he is giving half of his goods to the poor, and will repay those he has defrauded fourfold. The poor must have cheered—here is a man who is good news; he eats with the wealthy and they give half of what they have to the poor and restore what they have gotten by oppression. Jesus says, "Today salvation has come to this house, since he also is a son of Abraham." Jesus was good news for the poor and for the rich. But liberation and shalom justice have a price—some are willing to pay and some walk away.

Several of Jesus' teachings also reflect this good news. In 12:13-21, he tells the story of the rich man who stores up his prosperity for himself and his own enjoyment. Jesus pronounces this man a fool; he may be rich, but he is poor toward God. Following this, in 12:32-34, Jesus teaches his disciples to divest themselves and give to the poor and be rich toward God. Now anyone who goes about calling those who practice the economics of wealth fools, and calls on his followers to give what they have to the poor is good news for the poor. The poor listening to Jesus must have been saying, "Right on, Jesus, tell it like it is." However, for those mired in the economics of wealth, it must have been offensive to be called a fool for saving up for one's own benefit and security.

In another setting, 11:37-42, Jesus goes to the house of a Pharisee. Here Jesus upbraids him for practicing faithfully the religious rite of washing before meals while at the same time he is "full of extortion and wickedness." Jesus' antidote to this problem, is to give to the poor for "those things which are within; and behold, everything is clean for you." True religious cleanliness comes from aiding the poor. As in the case of the rich young ruler, Jesus is a problem for the religious wealthy, but good news for the poor.

In 14:12-14, Jesus has been invited home for dinner to the house of a rich man. Here in this context he has a lesson for his host. He says, when you want to give a big dinner, don't invite your rich neighbors, because they will just invite you back. Instead, invite the needy who cannot repay. In our terms, practice shalom economics where goods flow from those who have to those who do not have. Jesus finishes by saying, "You will be repaid at the resurrection of the just."

In all of this, it seems that Jesus' teachings would have been good news for the poor and needy, but a stumbling block for those of wealth and position. Some of these responded to Jesus' message of shalom justice, but others did not. Jesus was both good news and a stumbling block.

We can also trace this theme of good news for the poor and powerless in another aspect of Jesus' life: his concern for the socially oppressed and the outcasts. This comes through first of all in his association with women as illustrated in 8:1-3. But more than this, he affirmed the interest of women in learning. (See his interaction with Mary and Martha, 10:38-42.) From these brief examples, we can see that Jesus was a liberating force to free women from their normal social roles; he affirmed that they could be more.

Likewise, we see Jesus kindly inclined toward the Samaritans, the arch local enemies of the Jewish people. The classic example of this is the parable of the good Samaritan in 10:29-37. In 9:51-56, upon refusal of lodging for Jesus and his disciples, James and John wanted to destroy the Samaritan village. Jesus would have no part in this, but simply went on to another village after he rebuked them for their hostility.

The story of the sinner and the Pharisee in 18:9-14 illustrates Jesus' sympathy for the sinners: those who did not keep the law or keep it well. If they in humility asked for forgiveness, they would receive it, while those who felt that they had no need of repentance and forgiveness would not receive it.

From all these strands, we can see how Jesus as presented in Luke would have been seen as good news for the poor and oppressed, for those who were at the margins of society. Likewise, we can understand how Jesus was a stumbling block for the wealthy and religious elite, who could not accept this message of shalom justice—give to those in need, liberate those who are oppressed.

The structures of justice

In his message and matching deeds, Jesus brought the shalom justice for which the prophets longed. In this sense, Jesus was the messiah. Jesus also mirrors the message of the prophets in that he appealed to the elite and powerful (e.g., the rich young ruler and Zaccheus) to practice justice rather than proposing alternative structures to create justice. This did not mean that unjust structures did not need to change. Just as the prophets' message implied transformation, so did Jesus'. Shalom justice required structures of shalom to be put in place of systems of oppression.

It is important to understand Jesus' sayings as implying a social transformation since as long as we understand these sayings in isolation, outside of a social-structural context, we tend to dismiss them as hard sayings which we cannot practice in our world today. But we would propose instead that Jesus' words be seen against the background of the prophets: Jesus' message of justice continues their call and vision of justice. Just as their vision of justice was rooted in what we have called the economics of shalom, so, Jesus' teachings likewise should be seen against this background. Looking at them from this point of view, we find that these teachings are hard sayings from the standpoint of the economics of wealth, but make sense within the economics of shalom justice. Thus, *the teachings of Jesus need to be understood as calling for economic and social / political structures within which they make sense, or we are doomed to saying that Jesus' messianic mission is impractical and thus irrelevant!*

In order to see more graphically both Jesus' continuation of the prophetic call for the economics of shalom and how his teachings imply structural change, we will present again the chart on the economics of shalom justice versus the economics of wealth. This time, we will add Jesus' teachings discussed above by way of illustrating how they fit shalom economics.

The principles of the economics of shalom and economics of wealth

	Economics of Shalom	Wealth Economics
1. Ownership of subsistence resources	God owns, people use Lev. 25:14-17, 25-28, 29-31; Deut. 15:7-8	People own; exclude rights of others Isa. 5:8; Luke 12: 13-21
2. Access to resources	Open; gleaning, sabbatical laws Exod. 23:10-11; Deut. 15:7-11; Luke 6:30,34-35; 14:12-14	Closed, exclusive rights to owner; concentration of resources Isa. 5:8; Luke 12:13-21
3. Consumption	Based on need; wants balanced by surplus Deut. 14:28-29; 15:1-11; Luke 14:12-14	Based on self-aggrandizement Amos 6:1-6; 3:15 Luke 12:13-21
4. Distribution mechanism	Unbalanced reciprocity; based on need—from the haves to the have-nots 2 Cor. 8:14; Luke 6:27-36; 6:30,34-35; 12:32-34; 14:12-14; 19:1-10	Exchange for gain, based on getting more than giving; flow from have-nots to haves Amos 8:4ff; 2:6-8

5. Basic outlook	There is enough; trust and reliance on God 2 Cor. 9:8,10-11	Scarcity, so hoard; security is in saving for the future Amos 3:10; Luke 12:13-21
6. Basic value	Affluence is measured by leisure over against work for subsistence	Affluence is based on having more than others Amos 6:1-6
7. Disposition of surplus	To those in need 2 Cor. 8.14; Deut. 14:28-29; 15:1-11; Luke 14:13-15	Accumulate to support separate classes Amos 4:1; 6:1-6
8. Goal	Finite: the subsistence of all Deut. 15:1-11	Infinite; wealth, people never have enough Amos 8:5-6
9. Results	a. Stewardship of resources b. Redemptive justice, no oppressed or needy Deut. 15:4; Acts 4:32-34, 11:27-30; 2:43-46 c. Minimal force needed to maintain the system	a. Exploitation of resources b. Class separation; wealth in the midst of poverty Luke 16: 19-31 c. Oppression and increasing force to maintain class separation

As seen from the chart above, many of Jesus' stories and teachings are the logical outcome of the practice of the economics of shalom justice. For example, the teaching of feeding those who cannot repay you, the story of Zacchaeus, and the negative illustration of the rich fool all hinge around the principle of justice economics versus the economics of wealth: do goods and resources flow to those who are in need, or is the economics of wealth being practiced, where we concentrate resources for the benefit of those who control them without regard for those in need?

In light of this does it not make sense to say that *shalom makers are committed to work for structures which make the practice of Jesus' message possible?*

Love and shalom justice

For Jesus, the motivation of love is at the core of the practice of shalom justice and economics. In Luke 6:27, we find Jesus' command, "But I say to you that hear, Love your enemies, do good to those who hate you, bless those who curse you, pray for those who abuse you." Examples of how this love command might be carried out follow. Among these examples, illustrations from economics are prominent.

"Give to every one who begs from you; and of him who takes away your goods do not ask them again" (v. 30; unbalanced reciprocity).

"If you lend to those from whom you hope to receive, what credit is that to you? Even sinners lend to sinners, to receive as much again. But love your enemies, and do good, and lend, expecting nothing in return" (vv. 34-35a; again reciprocity without a view to exchange for gain as in wealth economics).

It is significant that these illustrations are given to show what it means to love the enemy in specific terms. For many people who take the New Testament's teaching on love seriously, enemy love means either loving personal enemies or national enemies—that is enemies defined in terms of those who we assume have hatred toward us or wish to do us harm. This understanding of enemy love tends to leave us paralyzed—how do we love the Russians or Albanians? In terms of personal enemies, we think of how we can be nice or kind to them, to return good for evil.

But in Jesus' teachings, enemy love is expressed in economic terms toward the poor and powerless—lend to those who don't have good credit and may not be able to repay you. Let those who have need take from you what they need. The love which Jesus teaches is love for the poor and oppressed through specific acts which address their material conditions of poverty and oppression. The economics of justice is the way of love—for both friend and enemy, because it models the love of God.

While the economics of justice is motivated by and models love, Jesus also teaches that the practice of shalom economics demands undivided loyalty. Jesus makes this point in Luke 16:1-13. Following the parable of the shrewd steward, we have the well known teaching—you cannot serve two masters—which Jesus applies to God and wealth: you cannot serve wealth and God at the same time. People must choose. We have either to choose God and shalom justice or the economics of wealth. We cannot have it both ways. *We cannot choose both God and wealth economics.* Thus Jesus urges people to consider carefully, to count the cost before they commit themselves, 14:25-33. There can be no looking back, 9:57-62.

We should note carefully the significance of the choice Jesus gives—God or the economics of wealth. This is a religious choice not just a matter of economic preference, for, as we have seen, the practice of oppression and exploitation is the practical denial of God—it is practical atheism. We have mentioned Luke 12:13-34 which also teaches this lesson; the economics of wealth leaves people bankrupt with God. The stories of the rich young ruler and Zacchaeus illustrate it. People must choose their sovereign.

The messianic kingdom

The call of Jesus was not only a call to shalom justice, but also a call to enter a kingdom. The Gospel of Mark presents the beginning of Jesus' ministry as a call to repentance and belief in the gospel because the kingdom of God has drawn near (1:15). Here Jesus' message was a challenge not only to change ways but to become a member of the kingdom. In this invocation of the kingdom, we find the *political* dimensions of Jesus' messianic ministry. He came to found a kingdom, but not necessarily a kingdom with territory.[5] Rather it is now a kingdom made up of those who would commit their lives to God and live in obedience to God's will as shown in Jesus' teachings.

Jesus' messianic rule now is not the reign of a king on a throne in this world, but a reign which is demonstrated in the lives of his subjects as they live out his call to practice economic justice and experience shalom. This kingdom presupposes the liberation of people from other lordships, so that they might be free to participate in God's kingdom.[6]

But is the kingdom really present in the world right now? Perhaps Jesus' teachings about kingdom living are not normative for us now because Jesus' kingdom is not here now. In fact, evidence can be found in the New Testament that the kingdom is not yet here. In Luke, we can point to 9:27; 21:29-32; 22:18 which talk about the kingdom as something which is coming or which is near. From these passages, we might conclude that we are to expect it in the future.

However, other references in the Gospel of Luke attest to the presence of the kingdom. For example, in Luke 11:20, the ability of Jesus to cast out demons was attributed to Beelzebul, the prince of demons. Jesus rejects this attribution and counters with the claim, "If it is by the finger of God that I cast out demons, then the kingdom of God has

---

5. E. P. Sanders, *Jesus and Judaism*, has persuasively argued that Jesus may have had two ideas of the kingdom—one for the present time of his ministry and one for the future when it would be fully consummated. This is helpful in reconciling the nonterritorial present state of the kingdom with the vision that someday there will be a physical kingdom as pointed to throughout the Bible.

6. A great deal has been written on the kingdom of God. Besides the scholarly treatments, I have profited from Carlos Abesamis, *On Mark and the New World / the Good News* (Quezon City, Philippines: Socio Pastoral Institute, n.d.), which treats the kingdom in Mark in the context of its significance for today.

come upon you." Clearly, the claim is that, in the work of Jesus, the messianic kingdom is being inaugurated into human history. Likewise, in Luke 16:16, Jesus points out that the law and the prophets were until John, but "since then the good news of the kingdom of God is preached, and every one enters it violently." Again the kingdom is beginning with the good news which Jesus is proclaiming. The content of this good news we have examined above.

So too, Jesus teaches that the kingdom is already among his followers. They should not, then, be misled by claims that it is here or over there (17:21). Or again, when Jesus is chided for not being more somber like John the Baptist, he replies that the bridegroom is now present and it is the time for joy and celebration.

Finally, many of the parables of Jesus seem to demand the presence of the kingdom. For example, in Mark 4:26-29, we have the parable of the seed growing secretly. In this parable, the seed is sown and grows of itself until the time of harvest. At the time when the grain is ripe, the harvest will come. We understand from this that the kingdom grows and is present in some way in the world. This same lesson is taught in the parable of the tares and in the parable of the drag net (Matt. 13:24-30, 47-50). Both parables assume that for a time, during the present, the kingdom and its members live side by side with those who are not of the kingdom. The final separation will be at the end, when the tares will be burned and the bad fish thrown away. Indeed, the latter parable closes with a specific reference to the end of this age and the judgment at that time. From all these many and varied witnesses, it seems clear that the kingdom was to be a present reality, beginning with Jesus' ministry; his deeds bore witness to it and his teachings were the laws of citizenship in it.

In this respect, Jesus fulfilled the second line of messianic expectation: he established a kingdom. However, contrary to these hopes, the kingdom was not one of political domain and territory. Rather it was a reign where those accepting God's sovereignty implement shalom justice.[7]

Politically, Jesus here seems to follow in the line of the prophets. The prophetic critique we saw was in part based on economic practices and the notion of justice. These two aspects of social life directly affect poverty and oppression. For a cure, the prophets did not dream up new political systems or options, but rather critiqued the abuses of the present system. Clearly, as we have argued, this was a call for social change, since, to remove these symptoms, a different economic point

---

7. The term "kingdom of God" is ambiguous. It can refer to a kingdom over which God rules, thus a realm or territory. Or it can refer to the rule of God, the kingship of God.

of view with the actual day to day doing of substantive justice was needed.

So, too, Jesus concentrates his teachings and critique on economic matters since these are crucial for the coming of shalom. To replace a Roman oppressor with a Jewish oppressor might do little for the poor and powerless. What was needed was not the exchange of one ruling elite for another, but a transformation of the society. Jesus did not call for rebellion against the foreign oppressor but his teachings to be practiced implicitly demand a real change of society at its grassroots so that there can be just economics and shalom.[8]

Perhaps a related argument may reinforce the point that Jesus' teachings call for structural transformation although he himself did not draw up any such blueprint. Healing was a significant aspect of Jesus' ministry. The church has followed the example of Jesus and has seen healing as important to its own ministry—many medical missions have been established by the church, for example. But how do these missions work? Do they only treat individual cases of disease, or do they also inoculate and initiate good public health policies in order to prevent disease? Obviously, they do the latter as well because through inoculation for smallpox, for example, they can make treating the disease unnecessary. Now, of course, Jesus never inoculated anyone, but if someone on that basis said they only treat diseases and not causes because Jesus only did so, we might think them misguided. So it seems with social diseases like poverty, oppression, and hunger. Since Jesus was concerned with treating these cases, why do we shy away from removing the social structural causes? Doesn't it make as much sense to struggle to transform the economic reasons for hunger as it does to eradicate the causes for smallpox?

Nevertheless, it is also true that the kingdom will not be perfectly realized in this world. It will not come *solely* through human effort. The witness of Hebrew Scriptures is clear, God's kingdom will be brought about by God's power. This is stressed in the parables mentioned above. The seed grows secretly once it has been sown. It bears fruit apart from human efforts. Thus kingdom members live in a tension between the call to be kingdom members and struggle for justice and shalom on the one hand, and knowing that their efforts will always represent an imperfect result of what should be. We can endure this tension because we know that kingdom work is also God's work. Thus kingdom members are co-workers with God. What they do makes a difference and in their working they do not work alone.

---

8. The classic book on the political implications of Jesus' ministry as well as of the New Testament more generally is John Howard Yoder, *The Politics of Jesus* (Grand Rapids: William B. Eerdmanns Publishing Co., 1972).

Entering the messianic kingdom

But in the end we seem to face a dilemma. Jesus called for repentance and entering the kingdom. But what he asked of people in order to enter the kingdom is not how we normally see the process of becoming a member of the kingdom. To put it rather crassly, was the rich young ruler asked to buy his way into the kingdom by distributing his wealth to the poor? Was the scribe, who was told to love like the Samaritan in the parable of the good Samaritan, expected to earn his way in by meritorious acts of love? The teachings of Jesus seem to leave out grace and belief, those things which we consider essential to kingdom membership.

This gap is especially felt when we read Paul in Romans, and elsewhere for that matter, since he places so much emphasis on justification by faith and not by works of the law. This issue comes to a head for us if we think again of the example of the rich young ruler—would he have gotten a better deal if he would have asked Paul how to be saved? Remember, all the Philippian jailer had to do was to believe. This seems to us a lot cheaper than giving our fortune away! In this section, I now want to turn to the issue of how one might put the teaching of Paul together with the teachings of Jesus.[9]

We begin by asking, what did it mean for Paul to become a Christian—become *in Christ*? Looking only at Romans 5—8, we can make the following observations. First, Christians have reconciliation and peace with God (5:1-11). This is accomplished by God through the death of Jesus. (Refer to our discussion on the atonement for further details on this passage.) Second, they have received the Spirit which both witnesses to God's love for them and guides them in their life (5:5 and ch. 8). Third, they are now part of a new humanity headed by Jesus the messiah (5:12-21), in opposition to the old humanity who are still following in the steps of Adam through whom sin came into the world.

9. My understanding of Paul has been formed by two works in particular: Krister Stendahl, *Paul Among Jews and Gentiles and Other Essays* (Philadelphia: Fortress Press, 1976); E. P. Sanders, *Paul and Palestinian Judaism: A Comparison of Patterns of Religion* (Philadelphia: Fortress Press, 1977). I will rely heavily on their views in what follows. By putting together, I do not mean harmonizing, although I may have fallen into that danger here. What I would like to do is show how the teachings of Jesus as they are presented by the Gospel writers and material which we have from Paul might be fitted together. This is not to argue that they are saying the same thing, but only that the things that they say may form some type of arrangement. I would also like to avoid in general what in my judgment are two extremes which are not helpful. One is to premise that if any two statements or texts by different authors can mean approximately the same thing, they do so. This I would call unwarranted harmonization. The other is to contend that if any two texts can be read so as to mean something different, they do so. This I would consider to be unwarranted disharmonization. Rather, here I would like to ask, what is a probable reading of the text and how does it pattern with other texts in the canon?

Fourthly, they are now under a new lordship, that of Jesus the messiah, rather than that of sin (ch. 6).

How is all of this achieved? How or by what process does this take place for the individual? Paul uses a variety of metaphors to talk about how we become part of the new people. Sometimes he talks about participation in Christ's death (Gal. 2:19-20; 2 Cor. 2:14-15). But often Paul uses the term *justification*. For some, this has become the dominant or only way in which becoming a Christian is described: we become part of Christ through the process of justification. In Paul, this term seems to mean that though once we were in bondage to sin and served as its slave, now we have been liberated from this bondage. Remember, sin for Paul is often those forces or powers which control our life, like materialism or feudalism. Liberation from these habits of thought enable us to have a new orientation, a new mind (Rom. 12:1-2). Thus *justification* is a positive term denoting both liberation from sin as a power which enslaves and service to Jesus our new lord. Romans 6 makes this point.

This doctrine of justification by faith has sometimes been understood as doing away with the law—faith in place of law. Paul, however, did not consider himself to be abolishing the law, but rather saw himself as placing it on a firmer foundation (Rom. 3:31). How is this so? The law as we have seen is a response to liberation. Biblical law is postliberation law. As a result, law, as we have consistently seen, is a response to God's grace. For Christians, it is the response to God's act of liberating them from sin; a response which enables them to be members of Christ and part of the kingdom.

In reading through Romans 2 and 3, it is easy to find what appear to be contradictory statements about the law. For example:

For [God] will render to every [person] according to [their] works (2:7).

For it is not the hearers of the law who are righteous before God, but the doers of the law who will be justified (2:13).

For no human being will be justified in [God's] sight by works of the law, since through the law comes knowledge of sin (3:20).

For we hold that a [person] is justified by faith apart from works of the law (3:28).

Do we then overthrow the law by this faith? By no means! On the contrary, we uphold the law (3:31).

How do we put together these seemingly diverse statements concerning the role of faith and the law. The key comes in seeing the law in its proper context—as following after God's grace and in its postliberation context. This implies that the law is not a way of earning grace, salvation, or liberation. It is rather the response of those who have already experienced God's grace and liberation. Thus the law cannot function in place of faith and grace in order to free us from the bondage of sin. That is, the law by itself will not cleanse our minds from the values of the economics of wealth. For this, conversion is needed—an act of liberation by God from our bondage to these forces of wealth which control our lives. It is this improper function of law that Paul is speaking about when he denounces the law and those who try to achieve freedom from bondage by doing it.

On the other hand, as we suggested in the chapter on law, once we have been liberated from wealth economics, its values, and structures, the law can work positively as an indicator of the type of values and social structures which we ought now to strive for. It is this positive value of law—not as agent of liberation, but as indicator of how liberated people ought to live—which Paul still values. Seen in a more future-oriented context, as in the verse quoted above from Romans, we are presently freed from sin and bondage by God's power; but in the future, we shall be judged by our works. As Sanders puts it: saved by faith, judged by works.

Liberation from sin, especially from bondage to oppressive economic structures, expresses itself in freedom to live out shalom justice in our lives. As Paul puts it in Galatians 5:13, we are called to freedom. Being liberated, we dare not slip back again into any yoke of slavery. Only this is not a freedom for self and anarchism, but rather a freedom to love and serve (Gal. 5:13-15). If we use this freedom selfishly, if we bite and devour one another as Paul puts it, then we are not free and liberated at all. Freedom and liberation in Christ, then, for Paul, meant freedom to love and serve the other which is the purpose of the law.

Since love motivates shalom justice and since the law informs us how to bring about liberating justice, love is now proclaimed as the fulfillment of the law. This teaching is presented in the Gospels as beginning with Jesus. (See Luke 10:5-28 and the parable of the Good Samaritan which follows it, for example.) It is echoed by Paul (Rom. 13:8-10; Gal. 5:13-15). It is found in James (2:8-17) and John (1 John 2:1-6; 3:11-18; 4:13-21).

In Galatians 5, Paul very nicely links the themes of liberation, love, and service as fulfillment of the law:

> For freedom Christ has set us free; stand fast therefore and do not submit again to a yoke of slavery (v. 1).

> For in Christ Jesus neither circumcision nor uncircumcision is of any avail, but faith working through love (v. 6).

For you were called to freedom, [people]; only do not use your freedom as an opportunity for the flesh, but through love be servants of one another (v. 13).

Bear one another's burdens and so fulfil the law of Christ (6:2).

Freed from the sin of wealth economics

For Paul, the Christian experience is one of liberation from the power of sin which holds humanity in bondage. This liberation is a result of God's love for us in Jesus. It is accepted by us in faith. Being liberated from old masters, represented both by values and structures which embody them, we are transferred into the body of Jesus Christ. We now have a new lord whom we serve. As a member of this body, of this kingdom, we now respond to God's love by loving others which fulfills the law whose aim is justice. Our love then leads to shalom, if our love, like God's love, expresses itself in substantive social justice.

If this is the message of Paul, why has faith as belief come to replace doing? It is interesting that Jesus calls for repentance and doing, not intellectual assent. If being in Christ is doing the work of love through shalom justice, why has the mission of the church been so little involved in justice? Is the agenda of the church that of the kingdom?

For now it is enough to assert that the message of Jesus which we surveyed in Luke is in line with that of the prophets. In agreement with them, Jesus promoted shalom economic practices and denounced the practices of wealth economics. Positively, then, the kingdom of God is seen in efforts for substantive economic justice for the underclasses. Further, this is also the witness of Paul. Although he uses different words, he stresses freedom for love which fulfills the aim of the law: shalom justice. One way, then, in which *shalom makers are about the work of liberation is by freeing people from the sin of wealth economics*, since as people are freed from wealth economics they can be free to choose God as sovereign and work toward substantive justice for the poor and oppressed.

10. *Shalom Making Today*

O
ur focus has been on understanding the meaning of shalom and how it relates to other key themes in the Bible. But we also want to help Christians find ways to work as shalom makers in today's world. I have assumed that you have been making these connections, carrying on a dialogue between the core vision of shalom and your own life as we have gone along.

Also, we have focused on the biblical material and have not offered specific guidance for action because peacemakers will need to decide what to do based on their own circumstances. We can give no step-by-step directions on how to proceed in such situations. What we have here is a biblical basis for reflection on those actions and a guide to further work.

However, now at the end of our course, it might be proper to consider several general issues which relate rather directly to the shape of our work for shalom. One issue concerns context; what about the church and shalom? Is the church the agency through which Christian people ought to work for shalom?

The second relates to tactics—what about violence? Is violence a way to gain shalom?

Church and kingdom

An old quip goes something like this: Jesus proclaimed the kingdom but got the church!

This short saying expresses two widely held opinions. A gap exists between what Jesus proclaimed—the kingdom—and what the church turned out to be. The other is that the proclamation of the kingdom ended with Jesus. The church, it is assumed, went on to other agenda.

But these impressions do not fit the church we find in the Book of Acts; there we see both the proclamation of the kingdom and the church modeling the kingdom in its own life.

In Acts, the expression *the kingdom* or *the kingdom of God*, occurs eight times. Not many, to be sure. However, it seems significant that speaking about and proclaiming the kingdom begin and end the book.

In Acts 1:3, it is reported that Jesus spoke the things of the kingdom to the apostles. The kingdom sums up Jesus' last teaching and concern for the leaders of the early Christian community. On this note, the ministry of the church began.

In the last verse of the book, 28:31, Paul is in Rome proclaiming the kingdom of God. The progression in Acts is from Jesus to Paul, from Palestine to Rome. But the teaching and proclamation remain the same. This placement of the term *kingdom of God* seems to show that for Acts it was an important part of the message and mission of the early church.

When we look at its use within the book, we find they too are important ones. In 8:12, the Samaritans believed the good news concerning the kingdom of God when Philip told them about Jesus the Messiah and healed some of them. This was the first mission of the church that reached beyond the Jewish people.

In 14:22, when Paul and Barnabas revisited the churches which they had just begun, they encouraged them by telling them it was necessary to suffer to enter into the kingdom of God. Evidently the kingdom and its entry was a significant part of their missionary proclamation. In 19:8, Paul begins his mission work at Ephesus by seeking to persuade the Jews concerning the kingdom of God.

Finally, in 20:25, on his way to Jerusalem, Paul addresses at Miletus the elders of the congregation of Ephesus. He reminds them that he has disclosed to them the whole purpose of God. He sums up his efforts as proclaiming the kingdom. In these four references, the kingdom or the kingdom of God serves to sum up the core of the proclamation of the early church leaders—Philip, Barnabas, and Paul.

In this light, it seems overly sharp to set Jesus apart from the mission of the early church with regard to the kingdom, at least as seen in Acts. In fact, the early church continued to carry on Jesus' concern for the kingdom. This concern was not only one of proclamation. If we look at its internal life, Acts shows the church modeling the kingdom way of life as well. The inner life of the church is depicted most fully in the early chapters of Acts.

> They met constantly to hear the apostles teach, and to share the common life, to break bread, and to pray. A sense of awe was everywhere, and many marvels and signs were brought about through the apostles. All whose faith had drawn them together held everything in common: they would sell their property and possessions and make a general distribution as the need of each required. With one mind they kept up their daily attendance at the temple, and, breaking bread in private houses, shared their meals with unaffected joy, as they praised God and enjoyed the

favour of the whole people. And day by day the Lord added to their number those whom he was saving (Acts 2:42-47, NEB).

> The whole body of believers was united in heart and soul. Not a man of them claimed any of his possessions as his own, but everything was held in common, while the apostles bore witness with great power to the resurrection of the Lord Jesus. They were all held in high esteem; for they had never a needy person among them, because all who had property in land or houses sold it, brought the proceeds of the sale, and laid the money at the feet of the apostles; it was then distributed to any who stood in need (Acts 4:32-35, NEB).

From these two brief summary sketches of its life, we see a united group of people who appear to be practicing the economics of justice. In this practice, we can see a close link between the teachings of Jesus and the church. Note also the phrase in the last passage, "for they had never a needy person among them." This seems to echo Deuteronomy 15:4 which promises that if the sabbatical year forgiveness of debts is enacted, there will be no needy among them. It seems that in these passages we have a link between the early church and the tradition which reaches from Torah, the law, to Jesus.

In concluding this brief glance at kingdom and church in Acts, we can say that the early church continued to proclaim the kingdom and tried to embody it in its own life—including the economic aspects which we have argued are foundational for shalom. An apparent implication of this is that *shalom makers should find the church a congenial home for both active shalom proclamation and the modeling of the message*.

Knowing the church as an agent of the good news and a living model of the kingdom brings us to another consideration: the relationship of the church to the state and other political and economic bodies. The church is presented in the New Testament as the living link to Jesus. He is presented as the head of the church (Eph. 4:15), its cornerstone (Eph. 2:19-22), and its foundation (1 Cor. 3:11).

Compared to the church, the state is ignorant, it does not know God's wisdom or purpose in history (1 Cor. 2:6-10). As a result, it is within the church that God's purposes ought to be seen most clearly and furthered actively in history. The church should not expect the state to decide how best to promote God's agenda, the kingdom, in history. This is the church's role.

But two qualifications enter here. First, it seems clear from the Bible that God is at work not only among the people of God, but also among those who do not acknowledge God. In the Hebrew Scriptures, we have Assyria, Babylonia, and Cyrus all seen as instruments of God's purpose in history—even though these nations and leaders do not know the God of Israel. (See Isa. 45:1ff. where Cyrus is even called God's messiah!) It would seem that the arena of God's action in working toward justice and shalom is not limited to the people of God.[¹]

While shalom makers may surmise that the work for liberation, justice, and shalom is enabled and fostered by the church, it can also be found elsewhere. Shalom making is broader than the activities of the church. If this is the case, should not shalom makers be discerning to see where in history God's liberation and justice is developing and seek ways of entering into that struggle?

Second, the work of the church has often failed to be about the kingdom and its good news. It has set up tight structures more often used for control than for enabling liberation and justice. In this respect, the church mirrors the society around it. This power structure makes it hard for the church to value the coming of freedom to the powerless and exploited. Indeed, it may even lead the church itself to become an oppressor.

This passion of the church for its own structure can be compounded by an undue concern for the life of the church and its religious functions. Church leaders and members focus on the maintenance and growth of the institution. Evangelism becomes church growth rather than the good news of justice and liberation. The needs of its members and its own institutional agenda consume the resources of the church that should have been expended in the liberation of poor and powerless people.

Indeed, the church, having failed to become good news for the oppressed, may at times even be bad news! It seems to be forgotten that God's kingdom is the message not the church's kingdom. The message is not the church. To put it rather baldly and perhaps badly, we need kingdom growth and kingdom good news, not church promotion and church growth.

Because of these two factors—authoritative institutional structures and an internal agenda—among others, the church at present often fails to hold out a vision of shalom or to work for justice and liberation. In this context, shalom makers may find the church not only lonely, but even an adversary.

---

1. For the difference in role and function between Cyrus and the servant in second Isaiah, see Millard Lind, "Monotheism, Power, and Justice: A Study in Isaiah 40-55," *Catholic Biblical Quarterly* 46(1984)432-46. The task of the servant for justice went beyond that of Cyrus.

The question of *tactics*

Given the vision of shalom as presented here, based on justice and the economics of shalom, how do we go about working to bring shalom to life? Undoubtedly, a variety of tactics and strategies might be used. We will not discuss them all, nor will we take time to explore any single one thoroughly. What we will do is suggest several ways which are used in attempting to change the present structures of oppression into ones through which or in which shalom might be experienced.

Let's remind ourselves again, if it is necessary, that shalom depends on proper structures. Therefore matters of individual charity and lifestyle, while appropriate in themselves, are not enough to enable others to have shalom. What is called for is structural, systemic social change. In this light, the question of tactics is: how do we change structures?

One way of working for structural change is through channels which are already in place in our present institutions. This approach is a time honored way in the West of trying to implement reform. In this tactic, faith is placed in the power of the ballot box or the judicial system to bring about change in policy and structure. It is here, at least in theory, where citizens can have their say about how things work in a society. For many thoughtful people in the third world, however, it has become clear that, in their context, elections are much more an exercise in covering power with a cloak of legitimacy than an instrument to give people a say in how power is wielded—to what end and for whose benefit. Many examples of this use of elections can be given from the third world.

Indeed this has also been my experience with elections in the United States. I recall quite vividly the first presidential election in which I voted. The two candidates were Goldwater and Johnson. For me the choice seemed clear. Goldwater talked of bombing North Vietnam and winning the war with no holds barred. On the other hand, Johnson was calling for greater restraint and spoke out against bombing the northern part of Vietnam. Since the bombing of North Vietnam would cost the lives of many civilians—as well as more general considerations—I voted, with conviction, for Johnson. He was elected in a landslide. Six weeks later, he bombed North Vietnam! The faces and rhetoric may change, but policies and the way institutions and structures work goes on.

The problem with the option of change within the system or structures is that the structures and institutions in place often operate to maintain the present system of stratification and exploitation. Since they are its guardians and they benefit from it, they naturally resist attempts to change it. Thus, while on the surface, change through established institutions and structures may be an attractive tactic, and even allowed for in theory, in the long run, little change may result. This caution does not invalidate this approach, but warns against over optimism and being co-opted to working *only* within the confines of present structural and institutional realities.

Furthermore, even if there was a clean slate, so to speak, and people could exercise a choice for various options, how wisely they would use this opportunity depends on the information available to them on which to base their choice. In many countries, the media is owned and operated by the government or controlled through censorship. In this situation, people come to believe a certain interpretation of how things are. This is even the case in countries with a so-called free press. What news is reported and how it is reported depends on the editorial policy set by the newspaper. At best, its readers get a screened version of the news. In this situation, people have little chance to make informed decisions and bring about real changes for justice.

Militant advocacy for liberation

Since structural change through present structures seems limited, it seems more hopeful to some to gear actions toward easing the worst features and effects of the present system. In this light, it appears to be a sensible strategy for shalom makers to engage in the politics of protest—to protest the abuses, especially the flagrant abuses of power and people to which the present structures are prone. The politics of protest means that shalom makers stand in solidarity with the victims of these abuses and try to defend them against the actions of those who have power. *This, it seems, is a necessary step in shalom making— identification with powerless victims of society and working to modify structures and institutions which adversely affect them.*

For shalom makers to identify with the victims of society will call for them to form friendships with poor and powerless people. Advocacy then becomes not some abstract political agenda or moral value, but an act of love done for a friend. Too often we talk about anonymous *them* or *they*, meaning those for whom we are acting. Rather, they and them ought to have faces.

Advocacy, however, is only a step because liberation is also necessary. Shalom makers must be midwives of liberation—helping the poor and the powerless chart and control their own future. Only when they are able to do this is the foundation laid for the experience of shalom.

This leads to the necessity, as we have argued above, of shalom makers actively resisting oppressive policies and structures. Civil disobedience is one way of resisting. It says, this policy or this treatment of people is wrong and we will not cooperate in this oppression.

Other similar ways of resisting and bringing pressure to bear on oppressive structures are boycotts and strikes. While they are perhaps not always as visible, they are ways which can be explored in an attempt to bring about change. It is in this arena that shalom actions affect lifestyle. As we order our economic lives to reflect the values of shalom, then our purchases for example are not based on economic factors alone, like price, but on moral and ecological factors as well. For example, usually when we decide on which product to purchase, we compare quality and price, and decide which one represents the best buy. From a shalom maker's standpoint, price is only one factor—the moral cost of the product and its ecological impact need also to be considered.

If these and similar measures fail to bring liberation and justice so that there might be shalom, then what? Violence? Revolution? These are words from which we almost instinctively recoil.

In order to put this option into perspective, we should recognize first of all that for most Christians now and indeed throughout history, violence was a viable option. The question was not violence, but its justification. In this context, since the church and the majority of its members have not been against violence, the question is *not* violence versus nonviolence, but *violence on behalf of whom or for what end.*

From our study above, it would seem that the strongest warrant for violence is liberation and justice for powerless and oppressed people. Perhaps even the only one. But it also seems at present in the West that it is exactly violence for this reason which causes problems for many Christians. Those who are willing to use violence themselves should consider carefully why this is the case. Why is it permissible for us to use violence—even the threat of annihilation—to maintain national sovereignty and power over other nations and to support and maintain oppressive institutions and structures within other nations for our benefit but inappropriate for oppressed victims to use violence for freedom, justice, and, in the end they hope, shalom?[2] It seems hypocritical to me for those Christians who hold the permissibility of violence to speak against it as an instrument for social and political change. And when they are profiting daily from violence inflicted on oppressed people around the world, it seems to me worse than hypocritical.

Further, we also note that shalom in the Bible was not necessarily the opposite of war, so we cannot simply appeal to the meaning of shalom as an argument against war, violence, and revolution. Indeed, in the Bible, warfare is one of the ways in which Israel experienced God's salvation. Military heroes in the Book of Judges were regarded as sav-

2. For a discussion of the legitimation of violence from a biblical and Christian standpoint, see Stephen Mott, *Biblical Ethics and Social Change*, chapter 9, "After All Else— Then Arms?" (New York / Oxford: Oxford University Press, 1982), pp. 167-91.

iors raised up by God. Thus the theme of salvation / liberation itself was closely connected at points with warfare.

Turning now to the question of whether lethal violence is justifiable from a Christian perspective and value system, it is important to recognize that I have not tried here to write about or describe the biblical teachings on the question of violence and nonviolence. It has not been my purpose to provide the foundations for a biblical pacifism. Nor is it my intention to admonish third-world people about violence—they have daily encounters with it. Rather I have been concerned with the topic of shalom and its connection with several other basic biblical themes and I have addressed these remarks primarily to a first-world audience in the hope of moving people from complacency to action since so much non-shalom begins here.

A major reason why I have not focused on the biblical basis for nonviolence is because many excellent books and articles on this topic are already available. On the New Testament, one can read with profit, *The Politics of Love*, by J. Ferguson; *The Politics of Jesus*, by John H. Yoder; *The New Testament Basis of Peacemaking*, by Richard Mc-Sorely; on Jesus and his teaching, more specifically, we have, *Christ and Violence*, by Ronald J. Sider; *The Nonviolent Cross*, by James W. Douglass. On the Hebrew Scriptures: *The Christian and Warfare*, by Jacob J. Enz. On the practice of the early church: *It Is not Lawful for Me to Fight*, by Jean-Michel Hornus. More generally: *Christian Pacifism: Fruit of the Narrow Way*, by Michael Snow; *Faith and Violence*, by Thomas Merton and *What Would You Do If . . .* , by John H. Yoder.

This is just a brief selection from the many titles which are available. From these books, it seems clear to me that the arguments for Christian nonviolence have been amply put forward time and time again. Let me say that, in my judgment, these books make it clear that the biblical teaching is that the Christian way is the way of nonviolence. Taken as a whole, the biblical teaching would stand against the use of lethal violence to bring about justice and shalom. Insofar then as we are basing our vision and tactics on the biblical material, our tactics ought to be nonviolent.

But it might not be out of place in a book dealing with the topic of shalom to suggest briefly, and inadequately, three reasons which are widely recognized why Christians ought to be in principle for nonviolence. The first is the teachings of Jesus and the New Testament on love, even love for the enemy. It seems basic to our findings above that love is at the basis of shalom justice—the substantive justice which sets things right so that people can experience shalom. This love is an indiscriminate love. It loves not only those who are friends but also those in need and those who are enemy. Indeed, as we have seen, enemy love lies at the heart of the atonement. This is God's witness through Jesus that we are loved by God. This message is found in Romans 5:1-11—peace results because God loved helpless enemies. In Matthew 5:38-48, we have a parallel action commanded for those who would enter the kingdom and be children of God. In love for our enemies, we imitate God's love for humanity. It is precisely in this love of enemy that Christian love, like God's love, is distinct from normal, standard human love; see both of the above mentioned passages for this emphasis. This love is basic in our Christian campaign for justice and shalom.

Second, is the example of Jesus' death on the cross. According to the Gospels, he did not defend himself. On the contrary, as mentioned above, he forbade Peter to strike a blow in his defense. His call to his followers is also to take up their crosses and follow him—for the one who seeks to gain his life will lose it, but the one losing it for Christ and the gospel will gain it (Mark 8:34-38). Jesus' death was consistent with his teachings.

Now in Jesus' teachings and in his death there is no hint that this was only a matter of strategy or tactics, rather than principle. From all that we can see, Jesus' teachings and death were grounded on principle— this is the way people ought to live and treat each other. See for example, the teaching and example of love for enemies; *it is grounded in the nature of God, not in pragmatic considerations.*

Third is the example of the church during its first three centuries. That the church was pacifist during its first centuries, seems to me, most easily explained as a continuation of Jesus' and the New Testament's teaching and example. The church was pacifist, because that is the message of Jesus and the New Testament. (See *It Is Not Lawful for Me to Fight*, mentioned above.) So too, as Christians today, if faithful to this path, we will also be a people of nonviolence.

To avoid a source of misunderstanding, it might be well to define what is meant here by violence. It is the destruction of another human being. This can be done physically through military violence for example, but it can also be done psychologically or structurally. It is also apparent that shalom as well-being, as right relatedness, and as moral integrity stands against violence of all types. Recognizing this, it is difficult in my judgment to argue on the one hand that shalom means the removal of violence and oppression and on the other that it is compatible with violence, can be brought about by violence.

The point of this definition is that activism and the use of force are not included. From all that has been said above, and indeed the major point of this book, is that *shalom making is active, it is struggle to bring about social, structural transformation.* There should be no compromise with the evils of oppression and exploitation which impoverish, make helpless, and destroy human beings. In this struggle, the use of force is legitimate and we have pointed to some ways in which we might exercise force to bring about change.

This, it seems to me, is a significant point because for many, especially those in situations of oppression, the argument about violence versus nonviolence is really understood as an *argument between those who actually are committed and working to change the structures of violence and those who only talk about it*. Openness to and support for armed struggle is equated with commitment to social transformation. This equation is unfortunate, but it exists and should serve as a challenge to all Christians to be credible. When people are starving, being tortured, raped, and executed by the military, and living without hope for tomorrow, right theology or ethics is a moot point for them—they need liberation. It is, I hope, the clear challenge of the present work that pacifists above all, since they are committed to shalom, should be actively and wholeheartedly engaged in an active, militant struggle for transformation so that the poor and oppressed might experience shalom.

In summary, while peacemakers may not accept the tactic of lethal violence as a tool for social transformation, there should be no doubt about their commitment to the goal of liberation and shalom as witnessed by their participation in the people's struggle for this transformation. This seems to me doubly true for those in the first world who would claim to be peacemakers.

Transformed people

Since I believe that as Christians we are to be committed to working toward shalom militantly, but nonviolently, perhaps several further observations may serve as a way of bringing to a close our journey through the Bible guided by shalom.

If, as suggested above, love is basic to shalom justice, then as we have argued, it seems that people, as well as structures, need to be transformed. Sometimes we may get so caught up in the need for structural change, that we slight the need for a changed consciousness, a new orientation on the part of individuals. People who are caught in oppressive structures need to be liberated from the values and perspective inculcated by these structures. The shalom maker, as a result, is involved in a mission of conversion—converting people to a new understanding and way of life. (See also Rom. 12:1-2.) This conversion, based on God's love for them in Jesus, frees them from old patterns of thought. As examples, we have suggested racism, sexism, and the values of wealth economics. This conversion, as we have seen above, also expresses itself by the practice of shalom justice and economics individually and the transformation of structures to promote and make possible this new corporate way of life.

Finally, since Jesus in his life and teachings embodied the good news of the kingdom, his example models the call to conversion and kingdom life. In the end, he did not use political power and violence to force this agenda. On the contrary, he went the way of the cross, the way of enemy love. We are exhorted to follow his example by Paul in his quotation of an early Christian hymn, Philippians 2:5-11:

> In your minds you must be the same as Christ Jesus: His state was divine, yet he did not cling to his equality with God but emptied himself to assume the condition of a slave, and became as men are; and being as all men are, he was humbler yet, even to accepting death, death on a cross. But God raised him high and gave him the name which is above all other names so that *all beings* in the heavens, on earth and in the underworld, *should bend the knee* at the name of Jesus and that every tongue should acclaim Jesus Christ as Lord, to the glory of God the Father (JB).

In the end, then, it seems that the way of love, even suffering love, is the Christian way which brings about shalom. For it is out of love which transforms and makes new that people become new and structures become life giving. Violence can repress people rather than renew them, can perpetuate power over people rather than empower them, annihilate them rather than convert them.

But we need to remind ourselves in closing that love becomes suffering love because love which leads to shalom is active, engaged love. Jesus suffered and died in part because he challenged the elite and their structures. So, too, if we struggle for shalom, we shall suffer because we are actively confronting and resisting the structures of oppression and working for the liberation of powerless and oppressed people. Shalom love is not love at a distance, not love in the abstract, not love in the rocking chair—it is the love of confrontation, of strike, of protest, and of disobedience to the structures of violence. Shalom love is suffering love because it is a love manifested in struggle and opposition; it is embodied in conflict with the forces which hold people in bondage. Shalom love is suffering love because it is militant love struggling for human liberation, justice, and shalom which is God's will for our world. Suffering love will not stop until this struggle succeeds.

May God's kingdom come!

Indexes

Abelard, Peter 59
Abiathar 90
access 37, 81, 88, 92, 111, 126
affluence 17, 111, 127
agriculture, iron use 89, 92
Ammi-Saduqa 96
Anselm 55
atonement 50, 52; and ethics 57, 69; and
    shalom justice 66; as expiation 54; as legal
    fiction 57; as ransom 54, 61; as
    reconciliation 54; as redemption 54;
    classical theory 60; God's justice 53; in
    Christ 57; individualistic 62; messianic
    view 63; moral influence theory 59;
    satisfaction theory 55; theories of 53;
    visible in the church 70
Aulen, Gustaf 60

Beatitudes 32, 123
beth ab 86
biblical theology 8
boycotts 141
bureaucracy 92

censorship 141
charity 38
christology 57, 62
church 136, 139; and state 138; as
    oppressor 139; growth 139; pacifist
    model 144
civil disobedience 101, 141
class 112, 127
classism 60, 66
commitment 57
community 81; and covenant 79
conscientization 58
consumption 111, 126
conversion 58, 145
corvée 90
court system 98
covenant 75; and community 77, 79; and
    death of Jesus 78; and law 78; and new
    identity 78; and shalom 76; New
    Testament 77
creation 26
cross, harbinger of hope 69

demonic forces 69
devil 61, 62
diatheke 78
discipleship 144
distribution 106, 111, 126

economics of justice 128, 129, 131, 138
economics of shalom 111, 124, 126, 127,
    140, 142
economics of wealth 111, 113, 124, 126,
    127, 129, 135, 145
eirene 8, 19; theological use 20
Enuma Elish 26
evangelism 139
Exodus 39, 40, 43, 53
exploitation 2, 127; as denial of God 129

faith 56, 133, 135; core of 7
force, legitimate 144; misuse of 112;
    monopoly of the state 112; use of 90
forgiveness 50
freedom 71, 134

gleaning laws 98
God, and justice 24, 41, 98, 118; and
    shalom 109, 119; love of 44, 56, 59, 67;
    reconciling 57; saving power of 65;
    vengeance of 35; wrath of 35, 56, 60
gospel of peace 20
governance, kinship 92; state 92
grace 44, 132; and obedience 73; Old
    Testament 72

Hammurabi 95
hassil 42, 43
healing 131
Holy Spirit 132
hoshia 41, 42, 43
hunger 131

idolatry 50, 107
incarnation 55
injustice 5
Israel 102; family life 86; kingship era 86;
    pre-kingship 86

Jesus Christ 136, 146; and new covenant 78;
    as messiah 63, 64, 121, 122; battle with
    evil 60; birth 120; body of 135;
    crucifixion 20, 53, 61, 62, 63, 64, 66, 132,
    144; death of 59; example of 82; good
    news to the poor 123, 124; life 53, 64;
    lordship of 133; ministry of 8; ministry to
    physical needs 122; resurrection 53, 61,
    65; stumbling block to the rich 124;
    suffering as model 57; teaching on
    economics 64, 128; teachings 62, 123,
    129, 135; temptations 64
Jubilee 81
judgment 15, 29, 33, 45, 80, 106, 108, 115,
    117
justice 8, 17, 18, 39, 85, 97, 103, 107, 122,
    139; and love 45; as fortunes reversed 31;
    as vindication 32; basic to God 25, 27;
    defined 33; distributive 36, 37; for the
    poor 33; God as model 28; judges
    oppression 33; kingly duty 95, 96;
    liberates 33; needy delivered 29; powerful
    restrained 29; retributive 34, 36, 37, 56;
    Roman ideas 54; unmerited aid 34
justification 20, 65, 133

king, and peace 117; as oppressor 99;
    responsible for justice 95, 102, 105, 110,
    115
kingdom of God 9, 64, 120, 123, 135, 136,
    137, 138, 139, 144, 146; entry into 132;
    God's work 131; messianic 129; political
    dimensions 129; present reality 129

kingship 85; reasons for 92; rise of 85; source 94
kittum u mesharum 96, 97

land, access to 98; exploitation of 110; ownership 79, 91, 110, 113; redistributed 81; terracing 88, 92; use of 110
law 8, 74, 95, 104, 133, 134, 138; and grace 74; and justice 71, 82; and liberation 71, 77, 79; and order 37, 112; as shalom justice 82; instrument for shalom 81; instrument of justice 74; postliberation 74; purpose for 79; reform 98; tested by justice 83
legalism 71, 75; mentality of 74
liberation 42, 43, 50, 53, 65, 71, 74, 75, 86, 104, 105, 120, 122, 124, 129, 133, 134, 135, 139, 141, 145, 146; from sin 69; politics of 115
lifestyle 92, 103, 140, 142
love 67, 128; and justice 45; for enemy 20, 65, 67, 128, 143, 144, 146; fulfillment of law 134; of God 144

materialism 66
medical missions 131
meshiach 116, 121
messiah 63; defined 116, 121
messianic hope 115, 116
militarism 6, 89; as idolatry 106; chariots and horses 90
mishpachah 86
mishpat 97, 118
missions 131
monarchy 102, 109
money redistributed 64, 81

nationalism 69
new humanity 132
new social order 67, 68
newspapers 141
non-shalom 143
nonviolence 1, 2, 143, 144, 145, 146

obedience 74; and grace 75; and reward 75; as commitment 83
oppression 3, 15, 40, 60, 86, 90, 103, 105, 127; by laws 105; mark of atheism 30; politics of 115; reasons for 30
order 96
ownership 78, 81, 111, 146

pacifism, biblical 143
Paul 54, 57, 64, 66, 73, 78, 82, 132, 134, 135, 137; teachings compared to those of Jesus 132
peace 65, 117; use in English 1, 10
political action 84, 140, 145
politics of protest 141
poor, charity for 98; God's concern for 80; identity with 123, 128, 141
poverty 3, 17, 131; cause of 110, 113
power, misuse of 110
priests 93
prophetic critique 102, 115, 117, 130

prophets 24, 85, 93, 99, 102, 135; false 13, 17, 18, 22, 108, 109; false and true 107

qatsin 87

racism 51, 60, 66, 145
ransom 50, 62
reciprocity 37, 38, 128
reconciliation 65, 132
redemption 50
reform texts 110
reform, economic 81; kingly duty 96
religion as conservative force 109
repentance 64, 129, 132, 135
resurrection 20
revolution 142

righteousness 26, 97, 117
rosh 87

sabbatical laws 81; year 98, 138
sacraments 56
salvation 8, 39, 53, 62, 65, 71, 120, 124, 134; as future 47; as liberation 52; as material 42, 46, 47, 48; as personal 52; as political 42; as shalom justice 43; as total 49; in Acts 47; in Paul 47; in the Synoptic Gospels 46; personal and social 68; shalom justice in action 39
sanctification 69
sarim 87
Satan 60, 64
saving souls 49
scarcity 127
security 111, 127
servant as messiah 118
service 134
sexism 51, 60, 66, 145
shalom, and law 98; and relationships 14; and security 108; as God's will 18; as good health 11; as justice 13; as morality 16; as okayness 12, 15, 69; as prosperity 11, 12; as safe and sound 12; as straightforwardness 15; compared to peace in English 13; defined 10, 144; love 146; positive content 13; things as they ought to be 21
shalom justice 39, 40, 56, 65, 76, 98, 105, 106, 121, 122, 124, 125, 128, 135, 143, 145; as judgment 45; unmerited aid 37, 43, 44
shalom making 5, 13, 69, 100, 127, 135, 136, 139, 141, 144; and law 84; goal 114; tactics for 22, 34, 36, 37, 45, 119, 140
shebet 87
sin 47, 60, 61, 66, 69, 135; as bondage 51, 133; as oppression 51; as personal 51, 52; liberation from 134; other words 50; what happened to 50
social change 51, 92, 125, 130, 131, 140, 145, 146
social justice 135
sodzo 46, 47, 48
soul 48
state 85, 102; agency for justice 109; and shalom 114; and social injustice 114; bureaucracy 89; centralization of 89;

controlled by elite 113; defender of status quo 113; efforts to reform 114; New Testament view 99; opposition to 113; origin of 112; responsible for justice 100, 113; role of 139; shalom 109; transformed 115
stewardship 110, 112, 127
strikes 141
structural change, reason for 114
structures more just 37
suffering 137
suffering love 146
Sumerian Kinglist 94
surplus 89, 90, 92, 111, 127

taxation 90

Ten Commandments 72
therefore pattern 71, 75; and covenant 77, 78
tithe 98
tsedaqah 97

urbanization 89, 91, 93

violence 1, 4, 6, 103, 107, 136, 142, 146; defined 144; roots in injustice 114

war 142
women's liberation 125
worship 49; response to grace 73

yeshu'a 42

Bible References

Old Testament

Genesis
9:17-20   29
15   77
18:25   24, 28
26:26-31   76, 77
26:29,31   13
28:21   12
29:6   11
37:14   11
43:27, 28   11

Exodus
2:17   41
2:23-25   40
3:8   42
3:7-10   40
12:27   42
14:13   42
15:2   42
18:7   11
18:9,10   42
20:1   72
20:3   72
21:1-11   104
22:21   79
23:9   80
23:10-11   111, 126
23:11   81, 98

Leviticus
4:3,5,16   116
19:9-10   81, 98
19:33-36   80
25   81, 98
25:14-17,25-28   110
25:14-17,25-28,29-31   111,
   126
25:23   79
25:35-42   80
26:6   13

Numbers
6:26   12
25:12   13

Deuteronomy
7:7-8   44
9:6   44
10:12—11:12   72
10:17-79   80
14:28-29   81, 111, 126, 12
15:1-11   81, 98, 111, 126,
   127
15:4   112, 127, 138
15:7-8   111, 126
15:7-11   111, 126
15:9-11   110
15:10   82
15:12-15   80
16:12   80
23:24-25   98

23:25-26   81
24:17-22   80
24:19-22   81, 98
26:1-11   73
28:9-14   82

Joshua
9:15   13, 76
24   72
24:14   72

Judges
3:9,15,31   41
4:6,10   87
4:17   13
5:16   86
6:14,36   41
6:19   86
6:24   86
6:30   86
6:35   87
7:7   41
8:9   13
8:32   86
8:35   86
9:5   86
9:16,19   86
10:1   41
10:17—11:11   87
10:18   87
11:31   13
13:5   41
13:9   86
13:15,19   86
15:1   86
16:31   86
17:6   93
18:14,22   86
18:21   86
19:1   93
19:16   86
21:25   93

1 Samuel
1:17   12
2:1-10   31
6:18   88
7:3,14   42
7:14   88
8   85, 113
8:1-3   113
8:3   93
8:10-18   94
8:11-18   99
8:12   89
8:14   91
8:20   93
12:9-10   43
12:10,11   42
13:20   89
14:23   41
17:18   11
18:5,22-24   89

20:6   88
20:21   13
22:2   93
22:2-5   113
22:7   91
25:1-11   113
25:2-13   93
25:10   93
26:24   42
30:27-31   88

2 Samuel
8:4   90
8:16-17   89
9:9-10   91
11:7   11
12:17   88
13:23   91
14:7   88
14:30   91
15:1-12   97
15:18   89
15:27   12
16:4   91
18:28   12
18:29   11
19:24   12
19:30   91
20:25-26   89

1 Kings
1   90
2:26   91
4:7-19   90
4:22-24   91
4:26   90
4:27-28   90
5:6-8   90
5:12   13, 76
10:26   90
10:27   91
22:27,28   12

2 Kings
4:26   11
5:19   16
5:21,22   12
9:11   12
11:4   76

2 Chronicles
15:5   12

Esther
2:11   11

Job
5:24   13

Psalms
3:2,8   42
7:11   33
9:3-4   29
9:7,8   26

9:7-8,20 33
9:8 33
10:1-2 29,30
10:3-14 30
10:11 30
10:15-18 30
10:18 33
11:1-9 15
13:5 42
26 33
33 26
33:5 26
33:6-9 26
33:10-22 26
34:6 41
34:14(15) 16
35:10 14
35:27 14
37:9 33
37:37 16
38:3 11
38:38 16
39:8 43
41:9 14
43 33
54 42
58:1-2 28
58:11 28
67:4 33
68:6-7 30
72 98,99,102
72:1-4 96
72:12-14 97
73:3 2
76:9 30
76:10 33
79:9 43
82 31,99,104
82:1-4 27
82:5 27
82:6-8 27
82:8 33
89 98
89:5-14 25,26
94:2 33
96:10-13 27
96:13 33
99:1-4 27
103:6 30, 33
105:1-45 72
105:5 39
109:31 30
113 31
113:5-9 30
140:12-13 30
140:13 33
146 34,99,122
146:6-10 31
146:7 33

Proverbs
16:12 97
29:4 97
29:14 97

Isaiah
1:10-17 105
1:17 104
2:2-4 18, 22, 117
2:6-8 106
3:13-15 105
5:7 104
5:8 111, 126
9:1-6 117
9:1-7 15
10:1-2 17,105
11:1-9 117
16:3-5 116
30:1-5, 15-16 106
30:12 107
31:1-3 106
32:1,15-17 117
32:16-17 14
40—55 118
41:2 13
42:1-4 118
45:1-4 139
54:10 13
54:13-14 14
58:6 122
60:17 14
60:18 14
61:1-2 122

Jeremiah
6:13-14 108
7:3-7 105
8:11 17
14:8 42
14:10-13 17
14:11-14 108
14:13 13
20:10 14
21:11-12 105
22:1-5 107, 114
22:1-15 15
22:3-5 105
22:13-17 15, 106
23:5-6 15, 116
23:9-40 109
23:7 108
27:9,14 108
28:8 108
33:6,9 12
33:14-18 117
35 113
38:22 14
43:12 12

Ezekiel
13 18, 108
13:10,16 18
34:23-24 117
34:26 13
36:29 42
37:22,24-25 117
37:23 42
37:26 13

Daniel
3:16-18 75

Hosea
10:13-14 107
12:7-9 105
14:3 106

Amos
2:6 104, 110
2:6-8 103, 111, 126
3:9-10 103
3:9-11 17
3:10 111, 127
3:14-15 110
3:15 111, 126
4:1 111, 127
4:1-2 15
4:1-3 103
5:7 103
5:11 103
5:18-20 103
5:21-24 15
5:24 103
6:1-6 110, 111, 126, 127
6:1-7 103
6:12 103
8:4 111, 126
8:4-6 103, 104, 110
8:5-6 111, 127

Micah
3:9-12 105
4:1-3 117
5:2-4a 117
5:9-14 106
6:8 24, 38
6:11-12 105

Haggai
2:21-23 117

Zechariah
6:9-14 117
8:16 16
9:9-10 117

Apocrypha

Wisdom of Solomon
6:1-11 99

New Testament

Matthew
1:21 47
5:3-12 123
5:23-24 21
5:38-48 144
7:21-23 83
8:25 46
10:13 20
10:34 20
13:24-30,47-50 130
13:53-58 121
14:30 46
26:28 78
26:47-56 64

Mark
1:14-15   64
1:15   129
4:26-29   130
5   47
5:23,28,34   46
5:34   20
6:1-6   121
8:34-38   144
10:45   54, 61
14:24   78
15:30,31   46

Luke
1:46-55   31
1:50-53   120
1:51-53   32
1:68-79   120
2:29-32   120
3:10-14,18   120
4:16-19   122
4:16-30   121
4:17-21   64
4:18-19   122
6:20-26   32, 123
6:27   128
6:27-36   111, 126
6:30   128
6:30,34-35   126
6:34-35a   128
7:18-23   122
7:50   47
8:1-3   125
9:27   129
9:51-56   125
9:57-62   128
10:5-9   64
10:5-28   134
10:29-37   125
10:38-42   125
11:20   129
11:37-42   124
12:13-21   124, 126, 127
12:13-34   129
12:32-34   124, 126
14:12-14   124, 126
14:13-15   126
14:25-33   128
14:32   20
16:1-13   128
16:14-15   64
16:16   130
16:19-31   123, 127
17:20-21   64
17:21   130
18:9-14   125
18:18-22   123
19:1-10   124, 126
19:45-48   64
21:29-32   129
22:18   129
22:20   78

John
3:16   59
6:15   65

9   34
9:3,4   34
14:27   20

Acts
1:3   137
2:42-47   138
2:43-46   112, 127
2:47   47
4:9   47
4:12   47
4:32-34   112, 127
4:32-35   138
7:26   20
8:12   137
10:36   20
11:14   47
11:27-30   112, 127
14:9   47
14:22   137
15:1,11   47
16:30,31   47
19:8   137
20:25   137
24:2   20
27:20,31   47, 48
28:31   137

Romans
1:7   19
2:7   133
2:13   133
3:1-8   35
3:20   133
3:24-26   54
3:25,26   35
3:28   133
3:31   133
5—8   132
5:1-11   20, 55, 65, 132, 144
5:5   132
5:6-11   56
5:9   47
5:12-21   132
6   66, 69, 133
6:17-22   57
8   132
8:2,39   57
8:6   20
12:1   73
12:1-2   133, 145
12:5   57
13:1-7   99
13:8-10   134
14:17   20
14:19   20
15:13   20
15:33   20
16:20   20

1 Corinthians
1:3   19
1:18   48
1:23   64
2:6-10   138
3:11   138

3:15   47
5:5   47
11:25   78
15:12-57   65
15:22   57
15:22-26   60

2 Corinthians
1:5-6   57
2:14-15   133
3:6   78
5:14-17   59, 66, 67
5:14-21   19, 78
5:17   57
5:18   54
5:18-21   57
5:19   59
8:8-14   82
8:14   111, 126, 127
9:8,10-11   111, 127
13:11   20

Galatians
2:4   57
2:19-20   133
3:13   54, 64
3:14,28   57
3:27-28   68
5:1-15   69
5:1   51, 134
5:6   134
5:13-15   134
5:13   134, 135
5:22   20
6:2   135
6:17   57

Ephesians
1:5-10   54
2:14-17   21, 67, 78
2:17   20
2:19-22   138
3:6   78
4:1   73
4:15   138
6:15   20
6:23   20

Philippians
2:5-11   146
3:10   57
4:7   20

Colossians
1:20   21
3:10-11   68
3:15   20

1 Thessalonians
1:6   57
5:23   20

2 Thessalonians
3:16   20

2 Timothy
2:22   20

Hebrews
9:15   78
13:20   20

James
2:8-17 134
5:15   48
5:20   48

1 Peter
2:9-11 73

3:11   20
5:14   20

2 Peter
3:14   20

1 John
2:1-6   134
2:3-6   84
3:11-18 134
3:23-24 84

4:7-11 67
4:10   59
4:13-21 134

3 John
1:15   20

Revelation
22   48

The Writer

Perry B. Yoder is professor of Old Testament at Associated Mennonite Biblical Seminary, Elkhart, Indiana. He received his Ph.D. from the University of Pennsylvania in ancient Near Eastern languages and literature. He also studied at Hebrew University, Jerusalem.

Before taking his present assignment in 1984, he taught at Bluffton College (Ohio) and Bethel College (Kansas). Between these two terms, he served for two years as People's Teacher of the Word, an itinerant mission of teaching the Bible in local congregations sponsored by Mennonite Voluntary Service.

For four months in 1984, he visited base Christian communities in the Philippines and entered into discussion and dialogue about justice issues. During this period, as well as during a similar visit in the summer of 1985, he tested and refined the ideas developed in *Shalom: The Bible's Word for Salvation, Justice, and Peace.*

Among other books that he has written are *From Word to Life: A Guide to the Art of Bible Study* (1982) and *Toward Understanding the Bible: Hermeneutics for Lay People* (1978).